Ambiguities of Activism

Routledge Research in Cultural and Media Studies

For a full list of titles in this series, please visit www.routledge.com.

Ambiguities of Activism

Alter-Globalism and the
Imperatives of Speed

Ingrid M. Hoofd

Routledge
Taylor & Francis Group

LONDON AND NEW YORK

First published 2012
by Routledge

Published 2016 by Routledge
711 Third Avenue, New York, NY 10017, USA

Simultaneously published in the UK
by Routledge
2 Park Square, Milton Park, Abingdon, Oxon OX14 4RN

*Routledge is an imprint of the Taylor & Francis Group,
an informa business*

First issued in paperback 2015

Library of Congress Cataloging-in-Publication Data
Hoofd, Ingrid M.
    Ambiguities of activism : alter-globalism and the imperatives of speed /
Ingrid M. Hoofd.
        p. cm. — (Routledge research in cultural and media studies ; 43)
    Includes bibliographical references and index.
    1.   Social movements.   2.   Anti-globalization movement.
    3.   Radicalism.   4.   Social media—Political aspects.   5.   Internet—
Political aspects.   I.   Title.
    HM881.H66 2012
    303.48'4—dc23
    2012002732

ISBN 978-0-415-62207-3 (hbk)
ISBN 978-1-138-64271-3 (pbk)
ISBN 978-0-203-10633-4 (ebk)

Typeset in Sabon
by IBT Global.

Contents

Preface

This book is the culmination of two decades of passionately attempting—by me, but also by many of my dear friends and colleagues—to bring alter-globalist justice to a currently unstable, oppressive, and violent world. I regard such a passion for justice as an important lifeline, especially in light of the growth of inequalities under neo-liberal globalisation, but also in light of the perplexities increasingly encountered in the course of my own alter-globalist activities. After having engaged in a manifold of activist and theoretical—and increasingly mediated—forms of resistance under neo-liberalism, one main perplexity started to foreground itself: how come there are so many good people fighting for a more just world, and yet the world does not appear to become any more just? Dismissing the too-easy answer that there must be greedy forces working against alter-globalism, I started to entertain the possibility that these activist and theoretical forms of resistance are possibly outdated, ineffective, or at least highly ambiguous today. New questions started to emerge: is there a relationship between our alter-globalist passions and the increasing desperation and disenfranchise-ment under globalisation? What are the intersections of left-wing activism with progressive theoretical work? How do new media technologies figure in this new problematic and in the aforementioned intersections?

This book tries to address these questions, and provide a tentative interpretation of the central predicament of our times for alter-globalists, whether they are at work in non-profit organisations, universities, or small activist groups. Let me use a note of caution here though: this book will not provide a simple road map or methodology. Instead, it tries to uproot certain petrified methodologies in popular forms of alter-globalist action and thought by way of rethinking the relation between activism and decon-struction. In doing so, it seeks to mirror the raised stakes for activism by exhausting to the point of *aporia* its own critical loyalty to activism's spirit. The book also does not seek to be comprehensive, but instead traces the contemporary problematic of alter-globalist justice back to a number of symptomatic nodes—new media activism, no-border activism, and climate change activism—in the wide present-day global matrix of new left-wing activism and intellectual thought. In this way, while putting contemporary left-wing thought and activism under a critical loupe, this book attempts nonetheless to remain loyal to the spirit that drives such activism: to bring about a better world. And precisely acting out this loyalty may paradoxically appear to be detrimental as well as our saving grace, as it consists of no less than the reincarnation of the promise of humanism.

I would like to thank all the activist, academic, and intellectual friends and colleagues in Europe, Australia, and Asia who have stood by me in the course of this process, and who will continue the quest for global justice.

1 Complicities of Resistance
Activism in the Era of Acceleration

Let us globalise the Struggle.
> Slogan at the D14 anti-European Union protests (2001).

Let's make things better.
> Philips Electronics global brand campaign slogan (2000).

Everyone resists, from gays and lesbians to rightist Survivalists—so why not make the logical conclusion that this discourse of resistance is the norm today . . . ?
> Slavoj Žižek, 'A Symptom—of What?' (494, 2003).

THE STAKES AND PARADOXES OF ALTER-GLOBALISATION

The world seems increasingly in dire straits where it concerns the existence and realisation of global and local social justice. Despite huge efforts to alleviate inequalities by many well-willing left-wing activists and academics, the world is seeing a rise in various forms of discrimination, widening gaps between haves and have-nots, environmental problems, and military violence. All these occur as an intricate part of the global spread of neo-liberal capitalism. Many, including myself, have spent a considerable amount of time and effort thinking through these problems and trying out various avenues of action that may successfully subvert or resist the dire effects of neo-liberal globalisation. A wealth of literature, from grassroots pamphlets to in-depth academic articles, has emerged over the last two decades that conceptualises, analyses, celebrates, or reports the progression of resistant voices and activities. New groups, projects, and formations have been and are continuously being set up to join the mission against globalisation. All these efforts seem laudable and necessary, to be sure. But a growing unease has been haunting these efforts, culminating in the baffling question: how come the world does not seem to get any more just or fair, even though so many good people like us are working or fighting for local and global justice? Is the inefficacy of our left-wing activism simply a matter of initially well-meaning activists and intellectuals being co-opted by ill-intended neo-liberal institutions? Are multinational corporate bodies and affluent people in positions of power within these bodies simply to blame for thwarting our efforts, or is the situation perhaps more complex?

This book claims that the situation is indeed much more complex and confounded. What is more, this book will argue that reassessing the grounds, aims, and stories of our left-wing struggles for justice is long overdue, as the stakes have shifted considerably after and due to the global information revolution. This book will also put forth the thesis that the best way to do this complex reassessment is through a renewed deconstructive analysis of the activism-capitalism-technology nexus. In order to first illustrate the perplexities of resistance against globalising forces, let me recount one of the memorable protests against globalisation my feminist-anarchist friends and I participated in, which took place in Brussels on December 14, 2001. Let the reader first understand, though, that I am narrating these events by way of recalling the *ideals* of activism and emancipation as I experienced and expressed them when partaking in these protests, but that I have since come a long way in understanding these ideals—which may to some seem naive or unrealistic—differently. The targets of the D14 protests, which were attended by as many as 70,000 people that day, were the latest legislative decisions of the European Union and its capitulation to the demands of global capital. We, the protesters, accused the European Union's new neo-liberal capitalist policies for aggravating the gender, race, and class gaps both within Europe and worldwide. We argued that these new policies would lead to an increasing feminisation of poverty and to the exclusion of ever more people from access to education, transportation, and new technologies. We understood policymaking within the European Union as an elitist practice, equal to exploitative corporate finance policies, and only favouring those people who were already rich, male, white, and comfortable. Since we felt that the corporate media were not to be trusted for much the same reasons, an Independent Media Centre was set up in a deserted cinema building in the centre of Brussels, in order to enable the protesters to make public the truth about the alter-globalist and libratory ideas and intentions of the D14. Word of the protests spread this way, creating alliances around the globe between us, the protesters, and others suffering from the global spread of neo-liberalism. But despite the huge protester turnout, we felt eventually defeated by the powers that be—the policies were not altered.

A few months later, though, in February 2002, some of my feminist colleagues and I were attending a European Union meeting on education and new technologies. I attended in the capacity of my post as a media project coordinator at a women's studies department of a Dutch university, which had hired me partly because of my knowledge of and ties to new-media and feminist activist groups outside the university, and I was ready to bring the battle inside. To my surprise, however, the questions addressed at that Union meeting turned out to be very close to my activist heart: how to bridge the gender, race, and class disparities in Europe; how to create access to education and new technologies through, for instance, online learning programmes for those who are disabled or who have no money to travel abroad to get a degree, and how to enable and increase physical student mobility and lifelong learning so that people get more opportunities to culturally and financially enhance themselves with knowledge and information. Most of the organisers of the meeting were women, and large sums of money were allocated during the meeting to tackle the issues discussed—all off which hopefully would create equal wealth and opportunity for all in Europe as well as in the long run for all worldwide.

What struck me at this point was that the Brussels protesters and policymakers around the vilified EU policies appeared to subscribe to the *same* ideals and goals—those of equal opportunity for all and of the eradication of class, gender, and racial disparities. Both camps also held firmly to the right to access and use of new-media technologies. The curious logic of this fight between protesters and policymakers, which was staged as oppositional by activists and the media but *was actually not* oppositional, repeated itself several months later in a public debate organised by a student activist group of which I was a member in my home university. We, the student protesters, accused the Dutch university rectors of having fallen for the evils of neo-liberal capitalism by signing the European Union Bologna convention—a convention set up to facilitate inter-university travel, third-party sponsoring, and international conversion of diplomas and grades. We positioned ourselves as students as the 'moral voice of the people of Europe' by asserting that what the university originally stood for, it should continue to stand for: the pursuit of untainted knowledge, truth, and reason as a moral obligation to liberate and empower *all* people. This was an obligation that should be carried out objectively, we said, and which should be disconnected from dirty politics, such as corporate economics. But interestingly, the rectors replied to us in desperation that the upholding and saving of the university's main function in society as a moral place in which the quest for knowledge and reason can continue was exactly what made them sign the Bologna Treaty and introduce third-party funding, so that especially the critical humanities could be kept alive.

I could cite many more examples of this recurring quasi-oppositional logic over the years that followed. The ongoing similarities in these struggles between the discourses of emancipation and empowerment employed by the surface disparate groups—the anti-EU and student protesters versus the university and EU policymakers—started to seriously perplex me. Both groups of people clearly operated with the good intentions of a democratising and empowering politics, seeking sincerely to help disenfranchised people. But the point of my recollecting these personal memories is not to simply dwell on my sense of bafflement. Neither is it to claim that alterglobalist activists are completely deluded in their stance against and critique of the European Union, nor that these European Union and university policies and decisions are actually benevolent. Instead, it is to introduce the reader to the likelihood that these similarities on the level of their emancipating desire and rhetoric may be structural to some larger global techno-logic, and that this has resulted in the distinction between whose claims are repressive and whose are actually helping those who are oppressed being increasingly impossible to make.

What I am suggesting is that nowadays many forms of alter-globalist resistance, in all their caring and fair intentions, are much more *in tune* with the underlying logic, norms, discourses, and values of those they view as their arch-nemeses than they tend to believe or perceive themselves. I will explain in this book why this is so, how this shows itself, and what the mechanics and stakes of this contemporary problem are, not only for left-wing activism but for the future of the world at large. This investigation into how such activisms potentially *comply* with exactly what they are dead set against should therefore be of interest to many alter-globalist activists and academics who have, since the start of such global protests, felt unhappy or uncomfortable about having to identify with certain groups within alter-globalism whose visions they see as antithetical to their own. For instance, many left-wing factions have great trouble walking side by side with extreme nationalist right-wing groups; eco-activists are disturbed by the many wasteful high-technological branches of the alter-globalist movement; certain feminist factions have problems with a number of Marxist groups for their continuing misogyny; global peace activists are anxious about the incessant participation of small numbers of protesters who use physical violence to show their disagreement with specific policies or to get media attention. I use the term 'alter-globalist,'[1] therefore, not only to indicate that most of the groups under this heading are not simply 'against globalisation' as such (the common denominator would rather be that they are against a Western-centred neo-liberal capitalist globalisation) but also to point out that what has been called 'the movement' consists internally of highly disparate strands. This internal incoherence, though, in which certain groups perceive other groups as counter to their own aims, norms, and values, gives rise to the suspicion that such groups are actually *not* as totally opposed as they initially appear. This is because *something* still seems to bind these apparently disparate groups together. This book hopes to shed light on the contemporaneity of this commonality and its problematic without rushing to the superficial explanation of some generalised post-modernity or paranoid empire.

A brief note on terminology here: I will use the term 'activism' throughout this book as a shorthand to describe a heterogeneous grouping of all kinds of anti-capitalist political practices in the 20th and 21st centuries that generally go under the heading of left-wing, pro-democracy, or alter-globalist activism. These more 'viral' groups, people, and projects of which I was and still am part, which in this book do not include those who go by the names of 'right-wing activism' or non-governmental organisations, and which sometimes come together at for instance the World Social Forums, are a good example of such activism. At times, though, I will also use the term 'activism' more ambiguously for certain theoretical practices within, for instance, academia, where individuals and groups exercise types of politicised activity using similar left-wing or alter-globalist ideas and utopias. It may be obvious furthermore that the term 'activism' relates somehow to the term 'activity.' This relationship, which harbours more than a semantic similarity, will allow me to delve deeper into the discourses of activism, its affiliation with forms of political thinking and theorisation, and its close ties with current neo-liberal economic arrangements. One main reason therefore to not look at various types of conventional identity politics (like gay-rights activism) or non-governmental organisations is that this book wants to look at those contemporary activisms that function on what is arguably a more affective level—a kind of 'viral' aspect of these prominent forms of practice that appeal strongly to and propagate an activist zest, identity, and *experience* like mine that is typical of increasingly global socioeconomic arrangements. In this sense, this book constitutes not a historical, sociological, or ethnographic study of present-day activism but engages with the activist question and its recent history from a critical and phenomenological perspective.

As the title of this chapter suggests, the main lens through which I will assess a variety of mobilised and theorised resistances is the lens of *complicity*. I will work this critical lens by weaving more straightforward critiques of activism with moments of complication, which allows me to grasp the ambivalences of contemporary resistance, as well as the at times uneasy connection between this book's own argument and left-wing quests for justice. This mix of critique and affirmation therefore emphatically does not mean that I dislike, oppose, or reject these forms of resistance, even though my tone may at times be critical. On the contrary, the activisms I will discuss have exactly made this book and its own appeal to justice and democracy possible. In this sense—and this is crucial—this book in a way continues the *spirit* of alter-globalist activism 'with a difference,' and is hence itself somehow also possibly a 'disloyal' piece of activism. But before the reader accuses me of misusing a term that designates a virtuous and bottom-up practice for an academic and elitist book, let me start by examining that illusive and illustrious term 'activism' more in depth.

COMPLICATING ACTIVISM, ACT ONE

The practices that go under the name of activism today are without doubt immensely diverse and heterogeneous. For the sake of grasping that what is typical of most contemporary forms of 'viral' left-wing activism in the phenomenological sense, this book will look at three types of alter-globalist activist projects that I have been and still am engaging in, and which have figured and still figure prominently in the larger European,

Australian, and North-American scenes. I have slotted these prominent activisms in the following categories for reasons that I hope will become clear in the course of this book: new media activism, no-border or migrant activism, and climate change activism. I will also look at how these activisms position themselves vis-à-vis the problems that they seek to solve or the institutions that they seek to contest. Whereas all these activisms do excellent work in the name of justice and democracy, I will nonetheless suggest in each of the chapters that the realization of justice—let alone the definition of justice—through these alter-globalist activisms is not self-evident. This is foremost because there exists in activist and academic circles working on social justice a significant lack of awareness of the concept of activism and its close ties to gendered, classed, and raced ideas of liberation, capitalist economics, and new technologies. This lack of awareness is particularly apparent in the disregard in many academic studies of the position that alter-globalist activism occupies in terms of mechanised economic *production*. I conceive of the term 'production' here as the precarious *re*production of hegemonies and their techno-material underpinnings, which relies on a discursive perpetuation of Eurocentric notions of what is progressive, valuable, and good, even if gender and race *seem* to matter less as primary nodes of struggle.

In short, one could certainly narrate the history of activism in terms of political dissent within nation-states, trace its current ideas back to May '68, or do a study of workers' unions.[2] But for the sake of focusing on an analysis of the *spirit* or *experience* of activism that suffuses many alter-globalist struggles today, I will suggest a particular etymology of the term 'activism' that immediately reveals a suppression at the heart of its currently too positive understanding in many circles. Activism and its basic traits encompass upon closer scrutiny a highly transcendentalist and economistic set of ideas. The term 'activism' was first coined at the turn of the previous century by the German philosopher Rudolf Eucken in his 1907 *Grundlinien einer neuen Lebensanschauung* (translated as *The Fundamentals of a New Philosophy of Life*). Eucken broadly formulated 'activism' as the ideology of energetic action which is required in order for humans to overcome what he saw as their 'non-spiritual nature.' His philosophy assumed the 'objective reality' and knowable relationships between the 'active existence of everything.' The term 'activist' became popular in English-speaking regions during the period of late colonisation and industrialisation of the 1910s and 1920s, and usually signified actions pursued in the name of a type of nationalist economic endeavour. German militant nationalism during the First World War, which sought to secure a rapidly industrialising German economy vis-à-vis its competing European states, was referred to in English texts as 'German activism.' During the same historical period, a branch within German expressionism with impact on the international art scene also went by the name *Aktivismus*. This strand, which sought to break with impressionism and pacifism, held that the purpose of poetry was to 'liberate mankind' and that the poet's chief role was to be an 'agitator' in service of 'liberation.' *Aktivismus* later morphed into the political realism of Bertold Brecht and others.

Eucken's idea about the merits of an active attitude to life was taken up by his son Walter Eucken, who used his father's notion of activism to formulate his theory of *freiheitlichen Ordoliberalismus* in his 1939 *Die Grundlagen der Nazionalökonomie*, translated as *The Foundations of Economics*. This economic theory inserted the idea of the 'freedom of the active and creative citizen' as essential for economic success so as to counter the depression caused by industrialisation. *Freiheitlichen Ordoliberalismus* is commonly understood as the predecessor of current neo-liberalism.[3] As a note on the side, this means that neo-liberalism has a decidedly liberal aspect which, I propose, draws on humanist ideals; neo-liberalism is then not simply *only* 'evil' as we as protesters deemed it to be.[4] The meaning of activism as essentially spurring economic activity for the 'spiritual good' of mankind and the nation also lived on for several decades in the German term *Aktivist* in former East Germany. *Aktivist* here meant 'a person who through a substantial increase of achievement and through new work techniques *speeds up production*' (my emphasis), while *Aktivistenbewegung* (activist movement) meant 'a movement that fosters the highest possible increase in production of a business' for the glory of the state.[5] So etymologically, activism has strong affinities not only with a transcendental philosophy of life, but also with nationalism and industrialisation. Activism was an economic strategy originally employed for the benefit of the nation-state in which its citizens could supposedly enjoy the largest amount of 'spiritual freedom' through actively encouraged but closely monitored economic competition. Activism was then the founding philosophical idea that allowed the implementation of a set of techniques and technologies—both material and immaterial—to increase economic production for the moral goal of mankind's emancipation. Not surprisingly, nationalists of former British colonies are in historical documents often referred to as activists, because they incorporated a similar technological, economic, and judicial method together with the concept of the free and active citizen in the newly decolonised nation-state. Nation-building was at that time essential for capitalist re-colonisation through expanding markets that went under the (false) header of decolonisation.

This modern rise of activism, which indicts it as a family member of neo-liberalism, becomes even more pertinent to this book's investigation into global justice when we consider that the discourses of activism and neo-liberal capitalism both employ a valorisation of productivity and progress. As such, individuals and groups are increasingly called upon to 'subjectivise' themselves and to 'take action' under neo-liberalism, showing its intricate ties to liberal and humanist ideas of 'freedom.' Under an activist regime, then—and I suggest our contemporary condition is such a regime—the citizen-subject is *compelled* to be active, creative, and free.

Any romanticisation of activism in turn uncritically accepts and repeats this essentially economistic theory of the subject and its technologies. The cry for activism and the compulsion to be active and creative obviously become even more crucial in our creative economy, which meritocratic underpinnings render it potentially even more exclusionary.

To illustrate how this curious collision of activism and neo-liberalism tends to appear in certain political and theoretical practices today, let me draw out the cry for activism and its relation to economics in the texts of two intellectuals who are relatively popular among contemporary activists in Europe and North America. Among the two texts, Tim Jordan's 'Ethics, Activisms, Futures' illustrates well the increasing importance put on activity and activism under neo-liberalism. Jordan, a staunch activist intellectual who has inspired many, argues in his chapter that activism is the new ethic for the near future. He sees the upsurge of activism as one that will increasingly undermine hierarchies because it will transform neo-liberal society into a 'movement-based society' (153). But in light of the connection between activism and neo-liberalism I sketched above, one will have to reassess the validity of Jordan's claim to this upsurge's undermining potential. A society based on a vital belonging to movements in which individuals can only stay alive by constantly pushing for their rights to the technologies of (neo-liberal) subjectivisation seems to me stressful, profoundly hierarchical, and resource-intensive. Jordan in a sense notices this problem when he discusses the negative consequences and ineffectuality of activist movements based on what he names the 'principle of (allowing for) differences.' If the adherence to difference, he claims, becomes the main tool for empowerment, then eventually 'difference no longer makes a difference' because the relationship between differences, and subsequently the production of differences, is no longer questioned. Politics will henceforth be conducted 'between splinters of essentially like-minded activists' (143). But Jordan does not elaborate upon the fact that such a post-modern politics of difference is hence at base a hyper-modern generation and repetition of sameness in which everyone must become 'like-minded.' What follows is namely the straightforward reproduction of difference as 'mere differences'—one that can be very profitable indeed for capitalist consumerism and its reliance on niche marketing and identity politics.[6]

Jordan tries to retrieve the inherent good of activism from its complicity with capitalism by contrasting it with the solipsism of 'pleasure-politics' which leads, according to him, to a 'disengagement from society' (151). But Jordan's division between activism and pleasure politics wrongly suggests that activism is never about pleasure. I insist instead, also speaking from my own experience, that most activism (and indeed, any form of altruism) is also about pleasure; it is in fact almost always self-centred or *self*-loving, because it seeks a replication of its worldview by including others in its strategy of action and alliance. In many examples of activist reasoning I will analyse in the next chapters, this element of self-interest—without which, I hasten to add, a reaching out to other people might not be possible at all—indeed emerges as a recurring theme.

The anonymous writer of the widely read and lambasted article 'Give Up Activism' about the June 18, 1999, protests in London[7] constitutes my second example. It was published in a journal with the telling name *Do or Die*, and aptly notes that being an activist is in essence the fulfilment of a role in society. As such, the writer argues, identifying oneself as activist indeed provides pleasure in the form of generating a self-image of being 'special' and of being at the forefront of revolution. But as the 'capitalist expert role' that it is, says the writer, activism must have its basis in the division of labour and thus in class society, and as such activism does not contest social hierarchies. S/he goes on to say that 'Activists would probably resist change because it would disrupt the easy certainties of their role . . . [Activism] has a certain attraction precisely because it is *not* revolutionary' (4, emphasis mine).

This attraction, I agree with the writer, is present in the practices I examine in this book because activism is paradoxically not revolutionary *in* its claim of being emancipatory. This suggests that its alleged radicality vis-à-vis neo-liberalism is a façade *in the service* of neo-liberalism. The writer concurs that the problem of the activist role is that it sees 'the Cause' as something *outside* of her activist self, and that activism fails to understand resistance as being done through (mostly capitalist) technologies of the self. Despite these lucid insights, the writer eventually recuperates 'real' activism just as Jordan did by suggesting that one can drop the performance of 'the activist' and instead work from an authentic position in one's quest for subversion. The result is that 'Give Up Activism' repeats the very position that it condemns. The article is implicitly also 'performing activism' while explicitly trying to distance itself from it. Its questioning quality nonetheless breaks helpfully through the self-indulgent image of activism—a sympathetic attempt at self-reflexivity rarely found in activist circles. I seek to take this critique mounted by this anonymous writer further.

I argue, then, that activism as the 'next ethical mode of society,' as Jordan envisions, will result in a new set of social stratifications—in congruence with activism's ties to neo-liberalism—that work in tandem with the technological *intensification* of social struggles under neo-liberal globalisation. In order to keep the dream of activist liberation alive, one must abandon anything that seemingly slows this process down—like 'unproductive' or deferring reflection. So the *aversion of (and for) deferral* is a central element of contemporary capitalism. Under neo-liberalism, one must become increasingly fearful or wary of 'not doing' and of not being productive in the call for progress and liberation, whether as activist or as academic, or indeed as a new global citizen. This is because delay or depression may and will cause one's own disenfranchisement. Being politically active then means less and less being politically *effective*—if we conceive of 'effective' as a mode that successfully contests the logic of late capitalism.

Thus, whereas Jordan sees the 'inability to come to conclusions and to close debates' (151) as merely negative, as activism 'gone wrong' (150), I suggest that activism's unintentional inability to close debates is precisely due to its insistence on justice.

All this means that alter-globalist activisms are exemplary of what drives an ever-increasing reproduction and acceleration of inequalities because of their global liberatory aspirations, their image of being the forefront of combating global inequalities notwithstanding. This essential *impurity* of contemporary activism may come as a surprise for anyone who is convinced of the univocal virtue of activism, or to anyone who believes it is better not to consider such ambivalences as it will hamper the work of emancipation. However, I maintain that activisms today revolve around a repetition of the fantasy of Eucken's subject-agent, which ties them closely to technologies of transcendence, communication, and production. As with 'Give Up Activism,' this problem foregrounds itself when claims are made that marginalised groups inhabit an oppositional subjectivity 'out there' in 'the real world,' or when the desires that foster change are represented as authentic to all humans; as if we are all 'like-minded.'

This means that the appeal to truth that activisms make needs to project some sort of 'evil' onto something or someone else that in essence resides as a tension *within* that type of activism. I will show in the next chapters that a projective 'self-righteous tone' is always *required* for activism to function, and that it is *there, at this moment of enunciation,* that its fundamental complicities arise. The rendering explicit of an activism's complicities therefore also shows which kind of historically specific *responsibilities* an activism carries forth, as if it were forced—by new neo-liberal techniques perhaps?—to do so. In any case, activisms are thoroughly implicated in humanistic and capitalistic discourses and technologies, and as such do not emerge from some abstract human craving for freedom or liberation as many liberal critics seem to think. This book therefore looks at the discursive mechanisms at work in the activist projects that repeatedly efface their being folded into neo-liberalism, an effacement that exhibits itself through a moral call for responsible action.[8]

Although my central argument, namely that we, as alter-globalist activists and academics either rallying or writing for social change and justice, are today labouring alongside the violence of globalising neo-liberalism, perhaps sounds a bit charged, I nonetheless invite the reader to consider her or his own academic or activist endeavours from this perspective. This consideration will show that much contemporary activism and left-wing theoretical practice continuously appropriates and repeats precisely those technological and humanist imaginations that underpin neo-liberalist globalisation. An obvious example of this would in fact be this book: the useful productivity of the notion of complicity points directly to the book's complicity in terms of its own production, never mind the vast machinery of the academic publishing industry that saw to its birth. This means just

as much that my book as well as these activisms may not repeat neo-liberalism in any knowable or straightforward way, and that there may also
be hegemonic shifts.[9] But as we will see later when discussing new media,
no-border, and climate change activism, such shifts will be necessarily limited and partial. All that remains is (my and our) humanist hope, without
proof. This, then, is the central predicament of activism at the moment: by
being compelled to hold on to emancipation in the unforeseeable future, it
sadly aggravates oppression today. It does this though, I claim, no longer
by way of above all benefitting those who bear the classical identity markers like masculinity and whiteness, but by feeding into the technological
production of a new global elite that runs across markers of gender, race,
and geographical location: the speed-elite.

THE RISE OF THE SPEED-ELITE

The enmeshment of ideas of economic progress with humanist notions of
justice has today resulted in an obsession, also among activists, with the
tools of progress and justice. This means that the problem peculiar to our
era that makes contemporary left-wing activism an increasingly daunting
undertaking are the current *technological* arrangements. I even go as far
as to suggest that new technologies as we know them today exacerbate
and intensify all of the above problems already present in activism, and
even introduce new complications. The general insight that resistance can
be complicit in forms of oppression, that alliances can be ambiguous, and
that activisms and forms of emancipation may entail a 'dirty politics', are
after all in themselves nothing new—a case in point being, for instance, the
role of the rhetoric of liberation under colonialism or American imperialism. What *is* new is how the current technological state of affairs results
in a situation where alter-globalist activism has increasingly *no choice* but
to *accelerate* neo-liberal production if it wants to keep responding to the
humanist call. The dominant discourses of technologies, and in particular the fantasies of 'freedom' and 'empowerment' that the new technologies promise under neo-liberalism, coincide increasingly with the humanist
fantasy of progressing towards liberation. By contesting the commonplace
idea in alter-globalist activisms that technologies are neutral or progressive
tools, ready to be appropriated by all, we can start drawing out how media,
transportation, and communication technologies aggravate the conundrum
left-wing activism finds itself in, and how this aggravation in turn feeds
capitalist over-production and consumption. Rejecting the assumption of
new and social media as neutral has thankfully started to inform some
recent research on activism, but often still fails to debate the role of the
media beyond issues of access.[10] Even Evgeny Morozov's recent *The Net
Delusion*, while providing some welcome criticism on democratic cyber-
utopianism, still conceptualises the Internet as at base a volatile 'empty'

space to be filled by the strongest force. Morozov hence blames the forces of profit and surveillance for overpowering the Net's capacity for 'freedom.' But he fails to see how this simplistic division, just as his rather muscular online performance of opposition against cyber-utopianist Jeffrey Juris—about whom more in Chapter 2—just as much contributes to this techno-logic of acceleration.

I will address the contemporary expressions of the humanist assumptions and particularities of new media technologies, besides the compulsive encapsulation of the other, from an angle reminiscent of Paul Virilio's *Speed and Politics*. I suggest that unearthing how new technologies are related to the reproduction of neo-liberal globalisation through activism lies firstly in acknowledging its technique and aesthetics of *acceleration*.[11] The current model of capitalism, which terms of production serve largely the 'speed-elite,' relies mainly on continuously extending and legitimising both the infrastructure and the neo-liberal discourse of the new information technologies. Capitalism has always done such structural crisis management by speeding up technological innovation, and thereby harnessing spaces and futures for economical growth and wealth accumulation for elite groups. Discourses that in turn typically get repeated in favour of the emerging speed-elite are those of connection, liberation, multiplicity, and overcoming boundaries.[12] Such discourses, which often build on technical spaces for action and communication between allied groups and corporations in order to formalise their repeatability, as well as on a rendition of the current condition as a stage beyond modernism, suppress not only the violent colonial and patriarchal history of those technological spaces and the subsequent unevenness of any such alliance. More severely, they foster an unacknowledged violent sort of unity of struggles and ways of being through the consumerist myths of allowing for differences and multiplicities, as we saw, for instance, with Jordan. The speed-elitist subject, who is an exponent of the Eurocentric humanist subject and is often prevalent in many forms of activism, can only handle radical difference by *incorporating* it in a grand humanist scheme of liberation. Such 'tension management' propagates the supposed neutrality or positivity of new technologies and the democratic ideal, but actually reconstructs and intensifies inequalities by virtue of a stratifying encapsulation. The result in alter-globalist activisms and in radical thought dealing with issues of disenfranchisement under glo-balisation is that those who are identified as the 'really oppressed groups' become the imaginary allies *par excellence*. These ideal allies become in turn the vehicles for the extension of the tools and discourses that facilitate this new speed-elite.

Speed-elitist global society is organised around the physical materialisa-tion of a desire for speed by way of modern technologies. This desire for speed is fundamentally related to the humanist utopia, because it is the subject's desire for emancipatory transcendence that revels in the logic of acceleration and its usurpation of space. In 'Chronotopia,' John Armitage and Joanne Roberts, for instance, recognise a 'chronotopianism'—the imagination of acceleration as segueing into a transcendental utopia just as Eucken may have envisioned—in the discourses of those who expand their businesses in order to generate 'opportunities' for others. Such neo-liberal discourses rely on fantasies of sped-up change through mediated connection and activity. But whereas managers and techno-happy intellectuals present this desire for connection as resulting in an open and creative space, its mode of production becomes exclusionary and violent. This is because it subjugates individuals under the hegemonic culture of spatial disengagement and meritocracy. This logic of speed, and no longer simply 'the West,' then makes up the current ideological centre.

The emphasis in speed-culture on constant *change* and creative action, which in turn leads to an accelerated production of information and technologies, is exactly the discourse through which neo-liberal capitalism expands today. This discourse is not merely the prerogative of corporate folk, but also highly present in alter-globalist activism and its emphasis on 'social change.' Speed-elitist discourses, I suggest, are just as much and perhaps even more present in intellectual and *activist* circles that try to imagine a unifying solution or equality for all through this techno-logic. One can namely identify in these often pro-technological and politicised activist arguments the implicit desire for an elimination of noise: the purging of any worldview that does not invest in this quest for social change. Ian Angus, for instance, in *Primal Scenes of Communication* likewise identifies in this purging of noise the fundamental aesthetic of neo-liberal globalisation, but he does not realise that this analysis points to a profound problem in alter-globalist activism. Quests for equality through the imagined positivity of technologies urge activists to work towards apparent laudable goals of 'access for all' or 'breaching the digital divide.' However, the overproduction that is the result of such endeavours facilitates the increasing investment into newer technological innovations. The money earned from the acts of 'including people' is used to accelerate the speed-elite even more and to disengage those who cannot keep up.[13] Speed-elitism is a downright dystopia when a multiplication of connection and a sense of being in the realm of new ideas enrich a happy few, yet result in an ongoing disconnection from this realm as well as a general impoverishment of habitations for many. It becomes imperative for individuals and groups to somehow plug into the subjugation that this imaginary provides, but such displays of empowerment cannot and should not be read as successful contestations or subversions as Angus does.[14]

The understanding of the activist quest as engendered *and* thwarted by speed-elitism sheds much-needed light on the *contemporary* conundrums and complicities of alter-globalist activism in neo-liberalism that have emerged from Eucken's philosophy. Activisms and the academic (social) sciences provide constant pressure and means for creative change, alliance, and knowledge production just like the speed-elite wants them to.

Furthermore, the imperialistic need for the elimination of noise that exists in accordance with speed-elitism typically results in a demand to remove (online) borders and boundaries. In spotting the discourse of acceleration in multinational corporations as well as in activist and liberal-intellectual groups, we can ascertain how these seemingly disparate groups are implicated in the same dangerous fantasy that remains unaware of its entanglements in increasingly violent conditions of possibility. Moreover, the repetition and acceleration of the increasingly desperate suppression and setting to work of humanist ideals through activist and corporate crisis management is particularly dangerous because the fantasy of crisis control remains exactly that: a *fantasy*. So this increasingly forceful repetition can only eventually give way to ecological and humanitarian accidents, because speed-spaces are fundamentally and exponentially unstable.

I would like to stress here that the repetition and acceleration through speed-elitism that activism complies with can never bring about an *exact* copying of the speed-elite's neo-liberal structures. It is the quality of difference in repetition, of the 'essential drifting due to [a technology's] iterative structure cut off from . . . consciousness as the authority of the last analysis,' as Jacques Derrida—about whom more later—would have it in 'Signature Event Context' (316), that allows for accidents and for *real* social change to appear. The difference through technologically sped-up repetition appears then as a *potential* or *promise*, but only as a growing potential or outcome that cannot be 'willed,' neither by corporations, nor by activists.[15] It seems that a displacement of the subject-as-agent is implied for activism.

The utopian fantasy in the alter-globalist activisms of a subject transgressing borders also sits eerily well with the rather Christian self-construction of many academics and activists as 'saviours of marginality'—Enlightenment and Christianity indeed having been strange bedfellows ever since European colonisation. The border-crossing faculties of new technologies in activist practice and thought appear much in step with American cyber-happy discourses on technologies, which makes one wonder how new or radical these practices really are. In fact, the rhetoric of radicality serves, I suggest, as a conjuring trick to pretend a break with industrial modernity and its ills. But actually, this trick makes one dangerously unaware how much of these modernist discourses and their material spread are repeated with such activist thought and practice. Activism thus regularly *dissimulates* the repetition of modernist ideals and ills, which is also why it makes more sense to talk of hyper-modernity rather than post-modernity as Jordan did.[16]

The influence of the media technologies on activism, quite contrary to what most academic literature on activism claims, is then one of increasing social entrenchment and division rather than of connection and liberation. What is more, new technologies have an increasingly displacing force to them because they produce ever more the *fantasy* or *presumption* of identity as something that is stably tied to a situation or location. This fantasy is an archaic one, and hence appears ever more as the grounding fantasy for self-determination. The usurpation of space by the speed of the new technologies therefore causes place or situation to become *spectralised* due to technology's *factual impossibility* of effecting humanist transcendence. Techno-economic power therefore not only carries global decisions, but new technologies are a main cause of the revival and entrenchment of archaic and modernist universalisms and essentialisms. A case in point here is the profound nostalgia for some lost 'nature' that suffuses much climate-change activism, in which 'nature' appears as a spectre from the past reprimanding us in the present. The rise of religious fundamentalism and nationalism provides also two clear examples.

In the final analysis, the material enforceability of justice[17] through new technologies enhances consecutively and exponentially the liberal and neo-liberal discourses and their exclusions that already reside at their base. As the temporal lapse of reproduction between socio-technological structures decreases towards near instantaneity, and incompatible or 'weaker' languages, cultures, and ways of being disappear, speed-elitism will become near-totalising. The structural accidents of such a totalisation are exactly those of the global feminisation of poverty, the condemnation of the slower classes to disenfranchisement, and the growing number of homeless or stateless people.[18] It will bring about a decrease in ecological and cultural diversity as well as a dwindling of sustainable production. The issue of ecological justice with its profound acceleration of the tension between the 'real' and the theoretical model of climate change therefore is a prime example of the extreme instability of speed-elitism.

With these words in mind, I understand what is called 'the information revolution' as a form of hyper-industrialisation, renewed through a sophisticated and technologically enhanced appearance. This does not mean that new media technologies cannot or should not be used as tools for resistance or subversion—in fact, they can very much be used for that, since our humanist responsibility increasingly works through the mobilisation of the technical realm. But such subversion is extremely limited because it suggests a repetition of neo-liberal logic embedded in the technological object and its discourses as well. I suggest that is therefore the *accelerated repetition of the suppression of the humanist aporia* and its violent patriarchal and colonial history that we are producing and enhancing in our alter-globalist activisms, through our beliefs, affiliations, and technologies, as much as 'it' in a sense produces 'us' and our arguments. And all this in order to keep the beautiful humanist dream of ultimate freedom, truth, democracy, and equality for all alive. But if it is already the case that our arguments are thoroughly wrapped up in speed, then how may *rethinking* the problem of activism, as this book sets out to do, help at all? What is to be done, if such academic activity repeats the belief in action through activism and its tools? To understand this and this book's strategy better, we need presently to mobilise this humanist aporia differently.

DECONSTRUCTION ALONGSIDE
ACCELERATION: A FATAL STRATEGY?[19]

In light of the complexities outlined above, I propose that there is increasingly only one perspective open to us if we want to elevate the alter-globalist project of justice beyond speed-elitism, namely that of *deconstruction*. Since this may seem to some perhaps absurd and/or elitist as deconstruction is for them merely a high-handed theory (and not a form of political action), let me start by validating my proposition by delving into the very idea and function of 'theory' today. This excursion will also show how speed-elitism is the productive logic underlying this book as much as it underlies activism. When it comes to theorisation and analysis done through what generally goes under the heading of 'post-structuralism,' 'deconstruction,' and 'critical theory,' many left-wing intellectuals rather unfortunately display knee-jerk reactions. Accusations of political relativism, in which post-structuralism is reduced to some caricature of 'post-modern theory,' emerge regularly from a variety of fields and persons who hold activism dear. One such example is Jeff Noonan's *Critical Humanism and the Politics of Difference*, which takes issue with what he perceives as post-modernism's political ineptitude. I am mentioning Noonan's book here because it is as deeply concerned with issues of global justice as my book is, but is nonetheless representative of the ways in which certain public left-wing or liberal intellectuals—I am thinking here also of the likes of Thomas Friedman or Martha Nussbaum—comply with the larger neo-liberal imperative by mobilising popular misconceptions and propagating a new moral universalism strangely at odds with the activist spirit that deconstruction inhabits. Through a minimal discussion of the work of Derrida and others, Noonan misunderstands deconstruction as a method that one applies to an object of study, and in turn blames 'post-modernism' for corrupting the road to justice. Since 'post-modernism' argues for a 'deconstruction' of the subject, we must instead, says Noonan, re-conceptualise the subject as innately desiring freedom and democracy, and chuck out post-structuralist ideas. This interpretation of deconstruction as method by Noonan is, I argue, emblematic of the tendency under neo-liberal acceleration to see anything in mechanical or methodical terms. Claiming that alter-globalist activism has been frustrated *by* post-modern theory—as if it was some kind of destructive instrument—is to utterly misidentify the source of the problem which thinkers like Derrida rather *mirror with a difference* through deconstruction. In other words, post-structuralism can show that the conception of the liberal subject of democracy and freedom is limited and historically particular *by critically affirming* it, thus laying bare humanism's aporetic structure.

The accusation of the political ineptitude and elitism of post-structuralism is in my opinion not entirely without ground, but this accusation may tell us more about the state of politics in general rather than identifying a shortcoming of post-structuralism itself—in fact, this is precisely the latter's point. Allow me therefore to explain how and why I will invite deconstruction in this book by delving into the internal logic of humanism that spawns such criticisms of post-structuralism. One may for starters wonder why these highly politicised, scathing, and eloquent critiques like Noonan's or Nussbaum's[20] of certain forms of *theorisation*, accusing the very field of being uncritical, relativistic, and apolitical, are above all produced by university-trained intellectuals in very nearly the same fields steeped in *theory*. After all, one would be hard-pressed to find a non-academic activist coming up with a strong critique of post-structuralism. I would argue that this paradox of humanists critiquing humanists is foremost due to the humanist intellectual and activist compulsion, bound up in their vocation, to appeal to the public—a public that is also the source of social inequality. The academic profession, much like the activist vocation, requires that it appeal to those outside academia through a narrative of morality that revolves primarily around humanist discourses of freedom, merit, economic and technological progress, and democracy. Therefore, the position of anti-theorisationism taken up by certain activists and intellectuals is in essence part and parcel of the intellectual and activist profession itself, and is as such implicated in speed-elitism. This understanding of what it means to 'profess' to the idea of justice and democracy conceptualises the humanist quest as *internally contradictory* and unfinishable; humanism inhabits a utopian vision, while it is this very vision which simultaneously calls for its own critique. Contra Noonan and many others, then, I claim that this humanist tension is precisely what deconstruction *inhabits*. Such an inhabiting also makes it *activist* (although perhaps beyond recognition)—after all, activism just as much builds on humanist ideas of freedom and emancipation.

So the analysis of this tension is crucial to better understanding the potentials and pitfalls of activism under conditions of acceleration. This is because, if we want to drive activism forward in order to make it catch up with today's raised stakes, we must first show how it possibly debilitates itself—in other words, we must look at its deconstruction. The first step is then to leave behind any superficial or starry-eyed idea of what activism is, while not dismissing activism outright; and I have started this trajectory by unearthing the etymology of 'activism.' I suggest next that the splitting off of pragmatic or activist ideas from elitist or academic theories, where activist practices are perceived as the producers of libratory thrust and where philosophy is described as useless, is itself a *product* of the *justificatory and reproductive function of this split under accelerated neo-liberalism.*[21] In fact, the blind validation of the inherent goodness of political action misses the reality of the activist creed running across the whole activist spectrum, from xenophobic nationalists to left-wing anarchists.[22] Such entanglements are similarly present in the institutions—be it the military-industrial complex or global multinationals—against which alter-globalist activism opposes itself or sees itself as outside of. What this means is that the action-thought dialectic is exponentially more set to work under neo-liberalism: in non-governmental organisations, research institutes, government bodies, consulting companies, and especially also in the numerous sociological studies that analyse activism. As this entails a fundamental aspect of humanism going into speed-elitist overdrive, post-structuralism is *the* theoretical attitude to show this problematic because it mirrors, exemplifies, and thematizes humanism's aporetic structure, asking *urgently* for its mobilisation to *slow down*. And deferral, as I suggested earlier, needs exactly to be activism's new ethical and political goal under acceleration. I want the reader to take note here that the inconsistency between urgency and its deferral is exemplary of the humanist aporia today, and that this tension therefore will return when I analyse climate-change activism.

Any simplistic validation of theory is itself of course also fraught with problems, and this book is necessarily caught in the tension between the two. The theoretical performance, which sets the conditions for me to study activism, relies on the presupposition that theory is independent from its object of study. Ultimately though, as many philosophers and phenomenologists have shown, it is not possible to discern neatly between a theory and its object, as theory is always engaged in the co-construction of its object of study.[23] Theory is then in the end an elusive concept, just as much one cannot 'do' deconstruction the way Noonan suggests—it is instead always already present in any political or analytical practice. The 'worlding of a world' in which activism is engaged is *as much a conceptualising* of the world as the 'theorising' that intellectuals are engaged in. The split between activism and theory that many social scientists assume, and the constant repetition of this split, is a *symptom* of a contemporary speed-elitist way of thinking in that it claims the concept of deconstruction as lying within the terrain of theory—and hence within high academic practice—*only*. This splitting off of activism as outside academia negates the fact that deconstruction is inherent in activist practices and vice versa whether they like it or not; the split suggests falsely that activism defines the authentic outside from which theory can infinitely derive its axioms.[24] It also suggests falsely that academic politics has no relation to its outside. The latter is, of course, typical of the popular 'ivory tower' accusation often hurled at academia by right-wing populists. But as this book also shows, nothing could be further from the truth: academic practice is profoundly political and steeped in internal contradictions (as also this book will show).[25]

So activism and theory are always intertwined. At the root of their relationship resides that ideology of the conscious and active *subject* as posited by Eucken, and its technocratic discourses that are culturally and historically specific of humanism that I argued now has segued into speed-elitism. They also believe in the humanist ideas of individual *intentionality* and social *progress* through knowledge production and the latest technologies as the proper road to liberation. Deconstruction is hence perfect for helping activism out by allowing it to unearth the raised stakes under speed-elitism.

What I suggest here is that these new activist stakes revolve around the impossible demand of conceptualising *action that must beget less action*. Judith Butler expresses this sentiment in 'Dynamic Conclusions' when she claims that 'it seems that the commitment to a conception of democracy which is futural, which remains unconstrained by teleology, requires a different demand, one which *defers* realization permanently . . . this may be a moment in which a self-defined activist ceases to read these pages, but I think that this insight is, in fact, part of the very practice of activism itself' (268). Deferral is therefore what may slow down speed-elitism, but what may just as much implicate itself in the mobilisation of the opposition between action and thought. By saying this, I do not at all suggest that being an intellectual is not a site of privilege—far from it. But I do suggest that this opposition is an effect of and feeds neo-liberalism, and that therefore activism as a rule entails a *considerable amount of privilege* too.[26]

COMPLICATING ACTIVISM, ACT TWO

If the aim of alter-globalism would instead be to *defer* the compulsion to be active, then activism and post-structuralism *must* be brought into dialogue today, even if this obligation to do so is also produced by the humanist imperative that inhabits speed-elitism. Proclamations of post-structuralism's nihilism or ineffectuality are, I suggest, part of an attempt to manage and eradicate 'noise' by the speed-elite. In order to show that activism and deconstruction are borne out of the same demand for *responsibility*, and to alert the reader to the difficult terrain this responsibility will land us and this book in, allow me to recall briefly Derrida's analysis of the very idea of *professing* before I move on to the three 'viral' activisms proper. In 'The Future of the Profession,' Derrida shows how the reproductive force of any ideology resides in the suppression of its internal contradictions. This suppression comes about through declarations of faith towards a certain belief system, which universalises such a belief system in order for the activist subject to self-actualise itself. What I take Derrida means is that we, as activists and radical theorists, *cannot help* but to *commit* to a historically and culturally limited perspective—like the speed-elitism we find ourselves in—whenever we act or speak majestically for 'justice and equality for mankind.' This is because this act re-constitutes as well as re-appropriates the humanist beliefs that ground academic and activist practice under speed-elitism. Derrida shows this by professing his allegiance to the humanities for being the one location founded on the 'liberating' notion of an 'unconditional freedom to question and assert' (24). His act of professing to the humanities, through asserting prime value in the practice of questioning, surprisingly opens up the possibility of questioning the humanities' unconditionality (of questioning). This is because the questioning and its supposed unconditionality are founded on the humanist ideal.

The productivity of the fantasy of unconditional questioning *must* therefore necessarily be the result of *a highly conditional situation*. It is Derrida's *performance* of his humanist belief of progress through unconditional questioning that shows that this performance relies on discursive and institutional constraints. The fundamental aporia at work under speed today resides between the *duty* to express the truth ever better and make mankind eventually free (which is indeed the general prerogative of activism) versus the *duty* to relentlessly offer space for critique of any appearance or teleological narrative of liberation or truth (for which post-structuralism or 'theory' is infamous).[27] In other words, activist freedom to critique, contest, or resist exists as a *consequence* of the constraints of the current institutionalisation, acceleration, and mechanisation of humanism under speed-elitism. The power *and violence* of alter-globalist activisms that base themselves on humanist ideals then lie in the repeated *suppression* by means of new technologies of this internal contradiction of humanism. Importantly, this suppression is also the one condition that drives these practices and institutions by allowing responsibilities to be taken, in turn making activism a pleasurable and meaningful exercise. The complication arises moreover that we increasingly do this through the *technologies of acceleration*. For humanism and its politics to keep operating, it must envision a utopian end that stands *a priori* in contradiction to its own specific grounds. The real reason for such a reproduction is instead the aim of neoliberalism to intensify and expand the market by increasing the number, frequency, repeatability, and formalisation of moral transactions typical of speed-elitism.[28] 'Freedom' and also the freedom to question therefore figure as a driving force behind acceleration. It is exactly this increasingly dissimulated deconstruction that only post-structuralism today can expose.

This perhaps seems all rather 'academic,' as the saying goes. Let me therefore provide a quick real-world illustration of this dangerous acceleration of humanism's internal tension. This illustration will also shed more light on the problematic yet productive tension between activism and post-structuralism that guides this book. As I mentioned, activism relies on the claim that it or its social problem resides in 'the real'—that it takes 'real action' as opposed to mere armchair theorisation. This *idea* of 'the real' exists nonetheless within the imagination of this claim (which emphatically does not mean that it is not true). Feminism, which bases itself on the notion of 'real women,' is a good example here that is again close to my activist heart. Although certain strands of feminism operate through holding on to the notion of 'real women' as somehow outside of or prior to languages, institutions, and technologies, the category of 'women' and 'their' empowerment can only be made possible by implicating itself in the languages and institutions that conceptualise 'women' as one different yet coherent group in the first place. Therefore, feminism is always a tainted politics: it needs to affirm patriarchy in order to be able to exist and appropriate its tools.[29] One could say that the fantasy of overcoming patriarchy is derived from the patriarchal fantasy of overcoming, as Elizabeth Grosz also proposes in 'Ontology and Equivocation.' A double affirmation is at work here: feminism must say 'yes' to patriarchy in order to affirm its utopian vision of overcoming patriarchy. This reinstallation is in itself not a problem—after all, this is simply how emancipation works. The trouble resides rather in how such a politics will become blind to what it reproduces, and which forms of exclusions these activisms aggravate due to such blindness.

The traditional idea of resistance, like 'feminist resistance to patriarchy,' which mystifies resistance as authentic, forgets that resistance is inscribed in the techno-logic of acceleration today. It is this *outdated notion of resistance* that returns in alter-globalist new media, no-border, and climate change activisms, due to an implicit allegiance to a sort of free-for-all techno-cornucopia, which gets mistakenly depicted as a break with old industrial capitalism. This fake break with old structures of oppression also figures in the supposed newness of the latest communication technologies, in which the superficial affirmation of differences à la Jordan, for instance through putting 'each individual's desires at the centre of technological experience,' is *technologically* reconnected under the sign of the same neo-liberal subject.[30] Therefore, when such humanist subject positions through technical spaces are increasingly what activisms use and re-create, then this field of deconstruction is exactly the one of empowerment. This implies that it is through the neo-liberal subject that the dream of emancipation is kept alive. A critique of activism must therefore destabilise the notion of the subject itself by gesturing beyond its conception as autonomous agent, and towards its object-hood. This utter blasphemy of the subject-as-object in the face of the idea of emancipation is exactly what post-structuralists like Baudrillard play on.[31] This means that the final dissolution of the subject into object-hood marks the end of speed-elitism while giving humanism new life, showing again how an extremely unstable state of affairs neo-liberal globalisation is.

To acknowledge such humanist ambiguity at the core of alter-globalist activism would entail not a loss of 'true' politics, as some would fear, but a gain. This is because deconstruction crucially unveils the contemporary limits, stakes, and complexities of liberatory struggles and their speed-elitist arrangements, and as such may gesture towards a radically better future. It is such radicality that politics today lacks. On another level, the acknowledgement of such complicities, and the exponential increase in their collision with globalisation through new technological conditions, may also point towards the urgent need to address the *sheer force* of current technocratic structures, as well as the growing potential for destructive accidents and structural violence that it perpetuates. Unveiling speed-elitism is therefore also important in the face of the new media technologies *obscuring* how that what we (as activists or as academics) enjoy doing affects others negatively. I am hence indebted to these activisms just as Derrida's allegiance in *The Ear of the Other*: that his critical readings stem from a strong love and concern for those texts, as for others generally.[32] My critique of activism that emerges in its deconstruction likewise arises from my love of activism. Deconstruction is never destruction, because it must *affirm* its object's premises before it can critique that object at all.[33] This 'loving' double affirmation means that deconstruction complicates the opposition between 'for' and 'against' speed: before one can either love or question, one must affirm one's condition. To show how deconstruction resides in a project is therefore an ambiguous expression of love for the *spirit* of that project.

So my 'deconstructive' critique of activism seeks to work alongside and develop the critical impulse and demands for justice that those activisms implicitly call for. More importantly, it wants to be an invitation for ongoing critical involvement in issues of global and local justice. Post-structuralism has ultimately something vital to offer to alter-globalist activism, namely a *resuscitation of activism's idealism* under increasingly oppressive conditions. Such criticism is unavoidably also self-gratifying—after all, it is this productive amalgamation of activist and academic work that advances my personal growth, and implicates me in the present historical, technological, and economical moment. Nonetheless, my sympathies remain thoroughly situated with these activisms, whose problematic underpinnings, in *the name of their own democratic spirit and their love for the other*, I nonetheless feel compelled to address. So my analyses of alter-globalism emphatically do *not* mean to spur on the traditional 'opposite camp' of left-wing activism (for instance, right-wing activism). Instead, it is the uncovering of the limitations of my double affirmation, and the impossibility of discerning to what degree such an affirmation is done out of self-love or out of love for the other, that hopefully opens my critique up for other loving 'left-wing' appropriations.

In claiming similarity between corporate and activist impulses, I do not seek to totally efface the differences between what is traditionally called left-wing and right-wing ideas. But I do claim that the closeness of such oppositional groups in alter-globalism points to the fact that the current moment has made the left-wing endeavour far more daunting than the old-fashioned idea of resistance to capitalism might have us believe. It may perhaps even no longer make sense to hold on to the term 'left-wing' at all. If it is apparently possible for both left-wing and right-wing groups to protest together under the banner of today's quintessential left-wing 'movement of movements' that the alter-globalist protest is said to be,[34] then left-wing activists need to look at what oppressive tendencies are present in their efforts that facilitate identification by right-wing protesters. In other words, I would like to make such conventional oppositions productive in a more unsettling, *loving*, and just way—the way of deconstruction. Since this book cannot—in fact, does not wish to—escape the humanist aporia, some of its argument may seem to produce inconsistent conclusions to some readers. But performing its humanist imperative *to the point of contradiction* is exactly its aim.

SPEED-ELITIST ALTER-GLOBALISATION STRATEGIES

In summary, we can recognise a number of *symptoms of complicity* within our activisms that emerge as the dominant strategies of alter-globalist activism and thought. I want to stress once more that activisms require these complicities in order to be productive or effective, but that 'effectiveness' can never mean full subversion of speed-elitism. Also, I forecast that the analyses in the next chapters complicate the sketched framework of the negativity of speed-elitism, as the central terminology of -isms and complicities will run into its own limitations. The first one of these symptoms is what I would like to call the 'teleology of progress' discourse. Parts of this discourse are taken for granted implications of breaking with industrial modernity, and the repetition of false oppositions like action versus theory, flow versus border, and nature versus culture. This discourse also spawns the outdated idea that resistance resides outside neo-liberalism, which results in modernist and romantic notions of liberation and 'freedom.' Next, such teleological narratives replicate themselves through utopian conceptions of new technologies and spaces for communication and action. This replication imagines technologies as value-free or open tools or forces as well as being a means to transcendence and overcoming boundaries. This technological discourse is related to the belief of the inherent positivity of the multiplication and enhancement of connections, which requires the forging of alliances under the pretence of allowing for differences. I will read in this forging of alliances under the pretence of difference a silent continuation of culturally and morally specific unification discourses. Examples are creeds such as 'everyone is a priori against capitalism,' 'everyone wants democracy,' or 'everyone is in the same way negatively affected by globalisation.' Speed-elitism's need for the replication of such unification discourses result in, and are a result of, the desire for 'saving marginality,' which tends to romantically perceive the margins—whether this concerns actual people or 'nature'—as inhabiting an authentic quality of subversion.

In light of the above, this book is relevant not only for those dealing with alter-globalist activism and for anyone interested in deconstruction, but also for scholars in media studies, feminist and subaltern studies, and new social-movement studies. Firstly, this study talks about activisms in terms of complicities, instead of the more widespread and less critical mode of analysis that studies activisms as successfully opposing, subverting, or resisting neo-liberal structures and institutions.[35] More specifically, this book regards the thoughtless repetition of activism as antithetical to post-structuralism, and as precisely (re)constitutive of speed-elitism. So rather than opposing rebellious agency to structures of oppression as many books in the social sciences do, my study analyses how such agencies work in tune with those very structures. This is also the reason why the book does not build its case around theories of economic globalisation and their activist opponents, but instead focuses on the issue of acceleration as the central under-theorized aspect of such globalisation.

Secondly, and related to this, this book integrates the analysis of activism with non-neutral theories of technology, instead of the more familiar discussion within and outside of academia of technologies as tools at the activists' disposal. What I suggest is that our current problem is far more daunting: namely that today, to respond to the democratic humanist call *has become* to technologically accelerate neo-liberal capital and its virulent logic of oppression. This problematic is unique to the present-day enmeshment of new technologies of communication, archiving, transportation, and representation, and the neo-liberal acceleration of capital. The apparent disparateness of the three forms of activism that this book analyses hence seeks to showcase the very ubiquity of this daunting situation. This in turn makes our left-wing claims and activities for emancipation today increasingly complex and possibly futile, unless we try to *slow down* so as to acknowledge and think through its complexity. Otherwise, the near future will most likely see a worsening of this trend. If one were to be unfriendly, alter-globalist activism fosters a neo-colonialism through pushing all these technologies of the speed-elitist subject. Simultaneously, however, alter-globalist activism, as it indeed represents our last hope for a more democratic future, exemplifies the intensification of the conundrum (and possibly deficit) of humanism. In any case, my analysis of the three categories of alter-globalist activism will show that the stakes have been raised considerably.

And finally, this book seeks to question its own performance alongside the complicities of the activisms under scrutiny, in preference to the common academic practice of simply invoking the researcher as the mastering subject and the activisms as the objects of research. Whereas this book thus sets out initially to critique various alter-globalist activisms, it will gradually move towards a self-reflexive critique of the humanist and technological assumptions and conditions that make this book and its argument for justice possible—especially regarding the paradoxical conclusions of the object-hood of the subject and the imperative to slow down. It is this self-reflexive approach without which any critique of activism becomes ultimately disingenuous and superficial. For instance, Morozov's *Net Delusion* notices the contradiction between governments heralding the Net while lambasting it at the same time, but fails to see how this contradiction is also present between the levels of condemning description and productive enunciation in his own book. My book's movement instead exhibits the continuum between resistances and institutions like academia, rendering false (but not equating) the opposition between researcher-subject and society-object.

This ultimately also renders false the opposition between the students-protesters and European Union or academic policymakers that I started this chapter with. The similarities of aims and rhetoric, which I discussed earlier, suggest that every activist claim to be on 'the oppressed' side, to 'really do' something about injustices, as well as the demonization of institutions as 'evil oppressors' or as merely elitist, whether this be the industry or the European Union, *marks exactly activism's complicity in such reproductions of inequality.* This is because such activism accuses those institutions of what activism itself (also) does. So then, in the cases of the examples of the D14 rallies and student protests, *the same technological and neo-liberal forces* that constitute the European Union make possible the very protests against the European Union, and the counter-voices put up by students and protesters reproduce the founding myths of the institutions they are protesting against. Perhaps, then, 'love' and 'justice' are themselves eventually at the heart of the problem of acceleration?

2 Tools of the Speed-Elite
Radical New Media Activism

> One thinks one is opposing Fascism, only to find that the identifica-
> tory source of one's own opposition is Fascism itself, and that Fascism
> depends essentially on the kind of resistance one offers.
>
> Judith Butler, 'Competing Universalities' (173, 2000).

> I must support them [Indymedia] because they are part of the hope
> for a democratic future. If they and institutions like them don't suc-
> ceed, this society is in deeper trouble than I like to think about.
>
> Ed Herman, co-author of *Manufacturing Consent*,
> to Theta Pavis (6, 2002).

FRANTIC HOPE, HIDDEN DESPAIR

The last decades saw a huge increase in the blending together of traditionally more local forms of activism—whether environmental, anarchist, democratic, feminist, or anti-racist—and the trans-national reach of new media
technologies. This enmeshment has proven to be particularly productive
between alter-globalist activisms and Internet technologies, and has given
such activism an enormous potential to reach out for like-minded folks
in other parts of the globe. Such opportunities for reaching out, compel-
ling many activists to *globalise* left-wing and emancipatory activities while
critiquing corporate globalisation, have encouraged many intellectuals to
theorise and co-develop the possibilities of emancipation through the new
communication technologies. Initiatives like the Independent Media Centres, the Association for Progressive Communications, GreenNet, and all
kinds of 'temporary autonomous zones' and new media activist conferences
sprang up as fast as the now infamous techno-bubble engulfed and globalised many local economies.[1] In tandem with these activist developments,
a host of academic and journalistic writing has appeared that largely celebrates new media and social media activism as successful forms of subversion of or resistance against neo-liberal globalisation.

But far from such endeavours actually subverting neo-liberal globalisation and corporate capitalism, this book suggests that there is a huge
problem with these activist uses and imaginations of liberation and of new
technologies. The synchronous rise and dissemination of these emancipatory practices and of the global spread of the neo-liberal market suggest an intricate relationship between the two. As I discussed in Chapter

1, this relationship runs primarily through the neo-liberal acceleration of flows. The activist aspiration or compulsion to globalise left-wing activism through new technologies is a product of and reproducing the increasing reach of neo-liberal globalisation, and in particular of globalisation's obsession with (the tools of) speed. This in turn makes left-wing claims and activities for emancipation today increasingly daunting, and demands that we try to *slow down* in order to acknowledge and think through this complexity—a thinking that must exemplify activism's deconstruction. In this chapter, I perform round one of this mode of thought by analysing several instances of new media activism. New media activisms comprise those types of political activities that foremost or exclusively take place online or through new media. Obviously, new media activism survives on an essential accelerating element of precisely that tool indispensable to the neo-liberal capitalist system it claims to subvert: new media technologies. Various media critics have indeed commented on the problems involved in understanding a movement as 'against globalisation' when it uses its primary tool.[2] But I would suggest that there is much more going on here than just an accelerating 'use' of those technologies, although this aspect is indeed an important facet of new media activism's problematic.

In the previous chapter, I conceptualised this interrelatedness of a politics of speed, connection, liberation and overcoming boundaries, whether pursued through business or activist endeavours, as the basis of a pervasive form of activities that I called speed-elitism. Speed-elitist types of activism increasingly disenfranchise many who fail to catch up with accelerated change, despite these activisms' wish to do the opposite. What is more, under speed-elitism's need for the production of excess, the areas of war, trade, entertainment, and emancipation have become almost completely interconnected, because all these areas mutually enforce each other through the usurpation and control of space (and territory) through the compression and regulation of time. The production of excess and the accumulation of wealth require this usurpation for the expansion of privileged peoples' spaces of pleasure.

This usurpation leads, I suggest, to a situation in which the most intimate and fundamental aspects of human social life, especially forms of communication and debate, become mere digits feeding incessant circulation and acceleration.[3] What this means is that speed-elitism engenders a violent destruction of non-commensurable idioms and ways of life under globalisation, resulting in turn in a compulsion, or fever, for what Jacques Derrida in his seminal *Archive Fever* has called 'archiving' such ways of life—to understand, preserve, and to finally encapsulate them. The futility of this archiving fever becomes clear when we consider that one cannot archive peoples or ways of life, since the technology renders what was once alive, 'dead,' or static. It is indeed regularly such a compulsion to archive anything 'other' to neo-liberalism that returns in many new media activisms, *as if* thereby its political potential can be harnessed. Such desperate activities, as we will see, appear as a *symptom* of neo-liberal capitalism's excess production through speed. And because of the relationship between militarisation and pleasure that such excess forges, we will also see that the discourses of warfare and 'fun' regularly find their way into left-wing new media activism. Cultural production through new media activism will increasingly find itself bound up in this speed-elitist logic.

Drawing out the discourses of acceleration is pertinent to an analysis of new media activism, but still leaves under-explored the question of how new media activism's complicity appears to be constituted in its *humanist potential* and imaginary through fantasies of progress, freedom, connection, and a generally emancipatory and democratic politics. Allow me to show the importance of this issue of *politics* for new media activism, which is central to the humanist imagination, through the work of political theorist and feminist Jodi Dean, who also tries to address the failure of new media activism to bring about true social change. Dean connects the logic of capital circulation to activist uses of new media technologies and the subsequent strengthening of neo-liberal globalisation. In 'Communicative Capitalism: Circulation and the Foreclosure of Politics,' she argues that neo-liberal capitalism should be understood as 'communicative capitalism,' as it relies on communication technologies for its production of excess. Under such conditions of possibility, communication—from setting up left-wing websites to participating in email lists—becomes more important as a generator of capital through its circulation, which in effect forecloses the possibility for what Dean calls 'real' politics. She points out that the ideas that underlie such capitalist expansion are the fantasies of participation, action, and wholeness, as well as 'technological fetishism.' The latter notion sees technologies as a fetish upon which the subject projects its 'hopes and dreams, with aspirations to something better' (63). Since such fantasies merely contribute to capitalist circulation, new media participation for Dean forecloses politics.

This is without doubt an argument that agrees to some extent with the one I make in this book. But while Dean's analysis definitely casts much needed doubt over the claims to justice of new media activism, I do not agree that such participation and action are not *political*. In its place, I would claim that 'real' participation and action through technological means is *exactly* political in the sense that it *reproduces* the humanist fantasy of technology as a progressive tool that underlies neo-liberal capitalism. It is telling that Dean, while rescuing the idea of Net politics as effective in certain circumstances and contexts, grants political efficacy to the B92 Net campaign in Serbia, because one could counter-argue that the B92 efficacy was a result of the expansion of neo-liberal capital into former Yugoslavia.[4] I thus understand the term 'political' as referring to the *active engagement* by groups or individuals in neo-liberal discourses and technologies, irrespective of whether such an engagement seeks to strengthen or subvert neo-liberal capitalism. In short, the fantasy is not that of participating, since one actually does participate by subscribing to and repeating the values of democracy, progress, and freedom. The main fantasy is instead that one's activist practice is largely autonomous, unrelated to the technologies one is wrapped up in, unrelated to neo-liberal power; instead, I claim that the desire to be politically active is today already subsumed under, and hence an effect of, speed.

It is therefore peculiar that Dean, in light of her lucid description of technological fetishism covering a more fundamental lack, eventually claims that 'Technologies should be *politicized*. They should be made to represent something beyond themselves in the service of a struggle against something beyond themselves. Only such a treatment will avoid fetishization' (66, italics mine). This is after all precisely what most alter-globalist new media activisms do through various forms of democratic imagination and action. So whereas Dean makes a number of interesting observations, like the prevalence of technological fetishism, I argue that it is precisely this re-politicisation by new media activists and theorists that allows for the fetishisation (and vice versa) of technologies. When Dean recognises, referring to Ernesto Laclau, that 'politicization [is] the difficult challenge of representing specific claims or acts as universal' (57), we can deduce that it is exactly this universalisation of humanist fantasies and values of progress—like democracy, autonomy of action, and eventually speed—which new and social media activisms adhere to that *is* the complicity that allows them to politicise issues. Her analysis thus repeats the speed-elitist compulsion of seeking once more an answer in the new technologies. Simultaneously, it appears that being political today means being wrapped up in speed, and that doing justice effectively also does violence. This shows the sheer displacement of good intentions and its relation to the quick dissemination of neo-liberalism.

The ways in which much activism today compulsively grasps new technologies as the road to emancipation is so profound that even critics of cyber-activism likewise fall in that trap. In 'The Daydreams of iPod Capitalism,' Rob Wilkie, for instance, argues that the fantasy that hierarchies (and in particular those of class) can be overcome by investing in the illusion of transcendence through cyberspace is wrought with problems. This is because it 'obscures that class is an objective relation' that has made and continues to make cyberspace possible in the first place (7). He notes that many new media activisms are in tune with corporate narratives of the Internet, and illuminatingly sketches how such a discourse serves the happy few who can imagine their actions as progressive because they do not suffer its grim effects. However, Wilkie's eventual call for returning the ownership of the tools of production—in this case, the industrial and information technologies—to 'the disenfranchised workers' represents yet another example of the extent to which the idea of technology as an essentially benevolent tool lies at the basis of neo-liberal capitalism as well as activist ideas of emancipation and liberation. It also shows how the forces of activism and capitalism, much like the seemingly opposite notions of war and trade, are in fact complementing each other. The existence of inequalities, dominance through technologies, and the pursuit of self-interest on the one hand, and the ideas of equality, progress, individual freedom, and democracy on the other, are nowadays treacherously two sides of the same coin.[5]

Therefore, whereas the analysis of how communicative capitalism renders the exchange value of resistances more important than their subversive content is useful for thinking about the (non-)impact of new media activisms, I nonetheless suggest that there is something more grave and complex going on. My issue with Dean's analysis of new media activism as part of capitalist circulation is that it renders this system of circulation as too stable and static a structure. This is because she depicts it as a system that manages to completely exclude politics. This full reproduction of speed-elitism by itself would be the kind of stability any ideological structure can only wish it had—an image of stability that appears as a result of Dean's and Wilkie's mythological repetition of originary desire that can 'politicise technologies.' It is instead the acknowledgement of the fundamental and exponential *instability* of the current neo-liberal system that today allows for the only possibility of a (democratic) event to come. So I would like to propose that the gravity of this complex situation lies in the fact that the technological acceleration of circulation is in *constant crisis*. The management of this crisis in turn runs through the tools and concepts of democracy. It is this humanist ideology and its acceleration that relegates 'less capable' groups which are historically female, non-white, and lower class to its margins. So we can expect new media activism to operate largely through a repetition of gendered, classed, and raced discourses.[6]

The fantasy that 'true' media activism resides at least partly outside contemporary economic circulation, which Dean unwittingly repeats in her nostalgic image of the governmental public sphere, is already an illusion in the function of the repetition of those historical inequalities. Such an illusion is vital to the speed-elite's 'fun' and empowering sense of control and mastery. Politics is therefore the *necessary ingredient* for the production and circulation of knowledge under neo-liberalism, as well as its constant crisis management. Dissent and difference, as well as the citizen-subject's compulsion to be political and responsive to the democratic call as if this response emerges from some innate human desire to be 'emancipated,' are required for speed-elitism to thrive. So when Dean perplexedly notes that 'organizing against and challenging communicative capitalism seems to require strengthening the system' (55), this is on the surface only a paradox of the more than logical cohabitation of a certain type of democracy, interactivity, capitalism, and speed. We can therefore safely conclude that the moment that marks the activism's complicity in neo-liberal globalisation is ironically that instant when it claims to effectively *oppose* or to be unrelated to multinationals, business forces, national government, mass media, and other such institutions.

In light of all this, I suggest that the continuous increase of information in our media-saturated society results in a *loss* of meaning because it exhausts itself in the act of simulating communication.[7] New-media technologies exacerbate the subject's *fantasy* of true communication with an 'other,' while increasingly what are communicated are mere copies of the same—a sort of general cancerous dissemination of the economistic conceptualisation of Eucken's 'active subject' which I introduced in Chapter 1.[8] In short, new technologies are the materialisation of that fallacy, and ensnare well-willing activists by way of the requirement of active political engagement to uphold that fantasy. This translates in a call to make oneself constantly heard and seen—to be vocal, to speak, participate, vote, disagree, decide, and in general to subjectively play out the humanist emancipatory promise.[9] The problem with new media activism is therefore not only, as Dean would argue, that their political counter-information means just more information and more capitalist production, but that it puts its faith in precisely those technologies and ideas of control, activity, communication, and of 'being political' that underlie the logic of overproduction.[10]

So in contrast with the quote from Ed Herman at the start of this chapter, I would like to argue that society's situation is in fact in deeper trouble than we would like to think about. In fact, the belief in providing a space within the Internet for authentic resistance that resides somehow outside neo-liberal power structures, which new media activism imagines itself to do, is problematic because it repeats the fantasy of the universal applicability of Eucken's *activist* subject working through his or her *technè*. This increasingly pervasive fantasy returns in many academic studies on new media activism. In these studies, the romanticisation of new-media alter-globalist actions as true agencies of progressive change works actually in favour of the reproduction of the opposition—equally complicit in neo-liberal globalisation—of activism and theorisation. So as a first step into the complications of new media activism, I would like to encourage the reader to wonder why considerations of 'deeper trouble' are often regarded as inappropriate in activist and academic circles, and how a marginalisation of these questions of complicity of activisms—which also takes place by way of ridiculing 'post-structuralism'—is key to speed-elitist types of production. In the end, what lies at the base of this speed-elitist production is a rather *desperate* upholding of the humanist utopia by (former) new media activists like me. This results in a constant techno-crisis management around this desperation, which causes a dissimulation of the problems and complexities of one's fantasies as well as of the negative effects of one's good intentions.

One of the most successful new-media alter-globalist initiatives of the last decades is without doubt the famous Indymedia project. The other reason, besides its prominence, for choosing to work alongside the tools, dreams, and desires of the Indymedia initiative in this chapter is that it provides an excellent example of the peculiar hybridisation and intensification of new technologies and alter-globalist struggles. Moreover, Indymedia's patent success by itself already shows that new media activism is indeed a close cousin of neo-liberal capitalism, rather than a successful countering force. Indymedia's success resides in the fact that it both sustains and produces a plethora of alliances between a host of left-wing activist struggles, in turn influencing the face of various worldwide decision-making processes like the G8 and WTO meetings, as well as research agendas of various academic institutions.[11] To historicise sufficiently my analysis of Indymedia, I will first look at the texts and ideas that inspired this project. I will also trace some of Indymedia's rhetoric back to various popular new media theories that preceded and accompany Indymedia—after all, as I argued in the previous chapter, theorisation and action are not disparate affairs.

TACTICAL MEDIA, AUTONOMOUS ZONES, AND DIGITAL MULTITUDES

The writings of various anarchist, environmental, and migrant activists, who were at the forefront of appropriating new media technologies, are worth considering in relation to Indymedia. This is because these activists and intellectuals were also at the cradle of Indymedia, and because their later activism and thinking are in turn informed by their experiences in projects like Indymedia. Of particular interest here are the ideas of activist-theorists like Geert Lovink and Hakim Bey, especially because they connect ideas of technologies and radical Italian notions of the multitude and the migrant, which I will elaborate further in Chapter 3.

Lovink's work is peculiar, because it often starts from a sense of hopelessness and from a lurking awareness of the ambiguities of new-media-style activism. But Lovink oftentimes appropriates such initial self-reflexive attempts in order to call for an appreciation of the next new features of media technologies that will make 'it' (that is, the complete liberation of mankind) magically happen. In 'Reverse Engineering Freedom,' Lovink and Florian Schneider, who is also involved in 'migrant' media activist groups like No-one Is Illegal and No-Borders, start with the bleak description of how lower-class workers in Romania lost their jobs because of outsourcing. Lovink and Schneider claim, however, that despite the increasing disenfranchisement of people under the 'fluctuations of just-in-time production . . . the Net still holds the capacity to articulate situated actors . . . [and] new socio-technical formations accumulate with unforeseen political force' (1). And although they claim that they do not want to provide an answer as to how to make this new political force happen, they readily conclude two paragraphs further down that the solution exists in 'numerous network architectures to be invented . . . We have to look at the next generation of *networking*, based on a culture of mutual *exchange* and *syndication*' (2).

Other keywords in Lovink and Schneider's work, which are likewise reminiscent of corporate speed-speak, are connectivity, invention, transformation, creativity, freedom, and especially the overcoming of social boundaries—all, of course, made possible by new technologies. The desire for all this 'newness,' sprouting from the 'discontent of millions' (2), is supposed to bring about a break from previous modes of capitalist oppression. Lovink and Schneider even claim that it will result in a revolution that will take the form of what they call a 'wikification of the world' (3). The desire from this multitude of millions and its quest for freedom must thus entail a desire to 'become the media': '[w]e are the media' (4), say Lovink and Schneider, or '[s]top downloading, start making news,' as Lovink repeats in 'The Technology of News.' Bafflingly, Lovink and Schneider do not see how the pursuit of such an imagination for the upwardly mobile like themselves (the 'we' and 'you' of the article) thrives entirely upon exactly the technologies of just-in-time production and the subsequent disenfranchisement of people like the laid-off workers in Romania whom they started their pledge for. They fail to understand the desires that drive these technological praxes as effects of those discourses of neo-liberal capitalism and its pretence of newness and progress. 'Reverse Engineering Freedom' therefore consists of a discursive *tour de force* aiming at generating (new media) activisms as exact mirror images of the discourses and tools of neo-liberal capitalism (like connectivity, mobility, creativity, freedom) through the complete *dissimulation* of relations of power. The slogan 'we are the media' depicts precisely the 'implosion of the social in the masses' (81) under hyper-mediated conditions, which also Baudrillard in 'The Implosion of Meaning in the Media' argues is happening.

Lovink and Schneider's 'A Virtual World Is Possible: From Tactical Media to Digital Multitudes' can in fact be read as a symptom of current left-wing *desperation* caused by the negative effects of neo-liberal globalisation—effects that these activisms paradoxically helped to facilitate. This desperation and hopelessness must of course be suppressed, or else the humanist ideal would fall apart. This suppression therefore leads them into arguing more strongly for recourse to those technologies that are already an intricate part of the humanitarian and ecological violence engendered by globalisation. The title of the piece in particular enacts an interesting rephrasing of the widespread alter-globalist argument 'another world is possible' into terms of desire for transcendence *into* new technologies. Lovink and Schneider talk nostalgically about 'the renaissance of media activism' and 'the golden age of tactical media' of the early and late nineties, which bound various movements worldwide together under the sign of the 'digital freedom of expression' (1). They acknowledge that this 'golden age' ran in tandem with the neo-liberal 'dotcom-mania.' They also admit that the demise of this mania signals an increasing awareness of how the intended erasure of global hierarchies that new media activism promised has not at all taken place. Instead, Lovink and Schneider correctly point out that ' . . . most movements and initiatives find themselves in a trap . . . we face a scalability crisis' (5). Although I remain sympathetic to the spirit in which they analyse the problem, I would counter that this 'trap' is not a scalability issue at all, but more an *accumulating sensation* of the humanist aporia due to acceleration. So rather than turning their gaze inwards in order to look at how their activisms have from the very beginning been 'trapped' in those very speed-structures they sought to contest and change, they counter this sincere feeling of crisis with a call for 'further mediation' and 'a rigorous synthesis of social movements with technology' (5). This compulsive repetition of calling for more of the same exemplifies exactly how the speed-elitist subject is always a precariously constructed prosthesis in service of the fantasy of a coherent identity: the fantasy of successfully contesting neo-liberalism that these activisms must uphold. This compulsion shows how Lovink and Schneider's point of view, saddled with the best intentions and lacking a clear grasp of why their subversions are not 'pushing through,' turns into a symptom as well as a cause of the mounting speed and spread of technocratic neo-liberalism. Their final fantasy, to 'install a virtual world' (4), is clueless about how this dream of transcendence for the new speed-elite can only mean increasing toil for many disenfranchised others worldwide, as well as an over-toiled earth. This is because it must rely on a heavily sped-up form of production as well as on obscuring such toil from the speed-elite's experiences in order to sustain the dream of such a virtual world. Many Indymedia activists echo this desperate push for acceleration. Sheri Herndon in an interview with Gal Beckerman, 'Emerging Alternatives,' for instance, claims that Indymedia should not merely 'slow the rate of destruction,' but instead 'increase the rate of creation' (9)—yet another argument for more speed.

The narrative of initial enthusiasm and subsequent despair is a common theme in Lovink's work, and I often experienced this circular sensation when working for Indymedia. It also emerges in 'Network Fear and Desires,' where he speaks of the 'unavoidable process of decay' (228) that set in after new media activism's initial glory days. Lovink tries again to enthuse his audience by proclaiming that 'it is time for . . . the genuine New that does not fit into the eternal return of the disappointment pattern, of being taken back into the System' (232). However, his smart invocation of 'the new' is exactly what signals such a quest's implication in 'the System'—the problem of 'decay and the being in the System' was already part of this desire for change through new media from the very beginning. Indeed, it becomes apparent from Lovink and Schneider's writing that there is increasingly no option left for resistance other than recourse to such technological imaginations. Lovink tellingly concludes 'Network Fears and Desires' with the declaration, which is meant to be romantic and tantalising, that the future will be 'hybrid . . . obsessed with progress, in full despair' (233). This utopia entails surely a dystopia for those who will be the ones actually despairing.

Lovink and Schneider typically claim that the old strategies of 'the left' have successfully been left behind. In 'A Virtual World,' they invoke Hardt and Negri's notion of 'the multitudes' as the liberatory constituent under late capitalism which coincides with a 'revolutionary being, as much global as it is digital' (4). The 'new subjectivities' that emerge due to migrant struggles and other border-crossing experiences are supposed to be exemplary of the subversive effects brought about by this multitude. As I will discuss in more detail in Chapter 3, this theory deceptively imagines border crossing and hybridity as a direct contestation of neo-liberal globalisation in itself. Such an imagination does not consider how such migrant fluxes are *produced by* and are reproducing global capitalism and its technocratic imaginary. Lovink and Schneider's fantasy that the multitude is both global and digital, and is *therefore* 'revolutionary,' repeats the bogus deterministic idea of new technologies as inherently liberatory. They even go so far as to claim that the concept of the 'digital multitude' is 'based entirely on openness . . . open sources, open borders, open knowledge,' without taking into account the extremely specific terms of negotiation that all these 'open' mediated spaces require. Their claims of total openness are therefore really empty rhetoric. Furthermore, they argue that this 'new movement,' whose practices comprise 'the Struggle,' 'works perfectly without an ideology' (3). But I would say that the pretence of having no ideology (or theory) can at base only be extremely ideological; an argument for 'practicality' that justifies the moorings of activism in an economistic social outlook.

I hinted in Chapter 1 at the fact that the new communications technologies allow for an even stronger acting out of the desire to imagine an idealised other. The alliance with this idealised other reconstitutes the new-media activist fantasy for liberation—it makes it whole and satisfies its imperialistic tendencies. It is for this reason that post-colonial critic Gayatri Spivak mentions in the 'Pax Electronica' interview with Lovink that she perceives computers and the Internet as an 'empirization of the desire for virtuality' (75). She even suggests to him that the Internet is an instrument of narcissism, because it pretends to reach out to the other where it actually does not; instead, it wraps the user up in reaching out for a similar kind of person who is then imagined to be a 'real' other. The computer is therefore for Spivak exclusivist, because this fantasy of reaching 'the' other, while borne out of a sense of obligation, is then exactly a withdrawal of responsibility. She goes on to say that the Internet is also exclusivist because of the 'stratification of the world . . . but that's another story' (75). But I would go as far as to suggest that these modes of exclusion are intrinsically related. The imagination of an ideal or radical other with whom one can connect through the Internet increasingly allows one to turn a blind eye to the larger global exclusions these connections require. Lovink hence does not get Spivak's hint, just as my fellow Indymedia peers remained convinced of the ultimate virtue of our activism. Even when Spivak later on throws into Lovink's face that '[it is] all about selling access to tele-communication-as-empowerment as such . . . global telecommunications combined with women's 'micro credit' is spelling out the importance of finance capital . . . [it] is a very scary thing' (77), he does not pick up on this clue. In short, Lovink's fantasy is upheld through the mental prostheses of 'new' subjectivity and technology. It is this complicit claim of subsuming all struggles under 'the Struggle against global capitalism' through new tech-nologies that allows one to 'become the media,' that also precisely traverses the Indymedia endeavour, as we will see shortly.

Similar to Lovink's recuperation of new media as essentially liberatory, Hakim Bey coins the famous notion of the 'parasiting web in the Net' in *The Temporary Autonomous Zone* to describe new media activism. Bey claims that the idea of a grand revolution is untenable in an era of high-level corporate globalisation, post-modern fragmentation of struggles along various axes of oppression, and strong Western military control (404). Instead, he visualises the 'temporary uprise' as crucial for subversion from the margins, and goes on to claim that the Internet lends itself perfectly for such a strategy. This is according to him because it allows for the fast creation and dissolving of alliances, which grants cultural counter-attacks a guerrilla-like quality. As we can see in Bey's argument, terms taken from conventional warfare are often used to describe new-media activist proj-ects. A very prolific term is 'tactical media,' which was abundantly used in the tri-annual Next Five Minutes festivals on media activism in which I participated abundantly. In 'The Language of Tactical Media,' Joanne Richardson traces the term 'tactical media' back to Michel de Certeau, who conceptualised the idea of the tactical against the idea of strategy. In De Certeau's view, a strategy is always a frontal assault of power or an institution done from a clear locus of identity, while tactics rather implies some sort of temporary infiltration and diffusion of boundaries—a more diffuse method of assault. Bey argues that it is indeed this capacity for dif-fusion and disappearance that makes the Internet useful for such activism of tactics. He notes that the new technologies have a strong 'repressive component' due to their military background. Nonetheless, he claims that many of their features, like speed of information and instantaneous con-nectedness, provide the means for an activist 'parasitic web' (the TAZ or 'temporary autonomous zone') which can be optimally exploited through temporal strategic alliances on the basis of shared moral goals (402). He thus coins the idea of 'the web' as some sort of autonomous and diffuse subversive element of the otherwise oppressive Internet.

The seduction of such a theory of the web is for activists like me of course irresistible. But what is interesting in Bey's terminology is his use of the notion of 'parasiting.' This term opens up his rhetoric to its decon-struction, and subsequently for a critique of speed. Far from the subversive connotation he seeks to aim for through the term, it rather suggests a more serious complicity. From an etymological perspective, to be such a parasite would entail 'eating at the same table' of 'Capitalism, Fascism . . . and the apparatus of Control, the State' (410, 433) of new media activism.[12] Such complicity becomes especially clear when reading how Bey imagines this supposedly subversive space. The two crucial stories that traverse the justification of the TAZ are those of the 'pirate utopias' and the idea of 'becoming Indian.' Bey writes nostalgically about the 1600s pirates, who according to him, lived 'outside the law' on a 'bit of land ruled only by freedom' (402). He even argues that

> Before you condemn the Web for its 'parasitism' which can never be a truly revolutionary force, ask yourself what 'production' consists of in the Age of Simulation. What is the productive class? Perhaps you'll be forced to admit that *these terms seem to have lost their meaning.* In any case the answers to such questions are so complex that the TAZ *tends to ignore them* and simply picks up what it can use. 'Culture is our Nature' . . . We are the hunter/gatherers of the world of CommTech. (411, italics mine)

This is unmistakably an unashamed refusal of any class analysis in the information age. Bey misrepresents completely the violent reality and the sexist, nationalist, and racist acts of such pirates, who were usually only regarded by their own countrymen as patriots attacking the ships of rival nations laden with gold obtained by colonisation. His idealisation of the pirate and hunter/gatherer is the mirror image of William Gibson's datacowboy in *Neuromancer*, the male lone rider pushing forward the new frontier of cyberspace. One may wonder which comfortable citizen can imagine class as being meaningless, and himself as a revolutionary cowboy, authorised to imagine that his own desires and imagination overlap '1:1' with the 'map of the Net' (410).

The idea of the 'new land' takes on grotesque dimensions when Bey connects his TAZ with the 'occultist operation' (!) that was the settlement of the 'New World' (418). These occult settlers were so generous (!) as to 'mix' with the local Indian population, and because 'the Indian' is 'Man' in the state of Nature, uncorrupted by 'government' (418), the end result was a community that in and by itself challenged relationships of domination. But this is utter nonsense: his exoticisation of the American Indian as having no culture or government in fact repeats the racist violence of their European colonisation. It also seeks to dissimulate the neo-colonialism that the concept of the TAZ, based on this utopia of cyberspace as empty land to be settled, exhibits in its desire to become 'the Wild Man' (423). Therefore, the opposition Bey creates between media activists and capitalists is not at all clear-cut. The antagonism between 'the (activist, parasitic) web' and 'the (corporate) net' is a falsification—they thrive on the same masculinist repetition of historical exclusions along race and class. Typically, therefore, Bey conceptualises the TAZ as a 'festival' (407), a tool for ultimately and instantaneously gratifying his quest for abundance and 'travel via the Net . . . facilitating my desires for food, drugs, sex, tax evasion' (417). If this is his revolution, it seems utterly unconcerned with looking at those structures of excess production that allow him to have increasingly direct access to what he desires, even if—and also because—his revolution pretends to be against neo-liberalism.

'The web' of new media activism is therefore not at all that autonomous space Bey describes it to be. We will see that this problematic notion of 'autonomous spaces' is pervasive in new media activisms like Indymedia. This again glosses over the historical structures of inequality, and the discourses and internal stratifications of communication that made such a 'space of instantaneous gratification of desires' possible in the first place. Speed-elitism indeed is a dystopia for increasingly many, since activism, war, and trade collapse into the intensification of inequalities around class, gender, and race. Eventually, then, one could argue that the perhaps well-intended 'guerrilla war' of the TAZ against capitalism and fascism is lost beforehand, because its technologies of language and production are already implicated in the neo-liberal logic of speed. Moreover, Bey's tactic of diffusion and disappearance through new technologies also demonstrates Spivak's point to Lovink regarding the withdrawal of responsibility through virtualisation, which problematically allows its users to be 'there and not there' at the same time—for activists a very attractive quality.

INDYMEDIA: THE PERMANENT AUTONOMOUS ZONE?[13]

> [Indymedia is] a network of collectively run media outlets for the creation of *radical*, accurate and passionate tellings of the truth . . . We work out of a *love* and inspiration for people who continue to act for a better world, despite corporate media's distortions and unwillingness to cover the efforts to *free* humanity.
>
> In *The IMC—A New Model.* (2004, italics mine)

Let me now draw out how speed-elitist discourses, their crisis management, and the intensification of the humanist aporia, which compels us to do politics with ever more vigour and complicit desperation, saturates a project like Indymedia. The basic goal of Indymedia, as we can read in its many online manifestos and mission statements, is to be an open space for all left-wing activists to 'publish, ally and connect' (Pittsburgh Indymedia, 2007; Germany Indymedia, 2000). It does this in optimistic resistance to the assumed monopoly and corruption of the corporate media, which in Indymedia's eyes only publishes news that is in corporate interests (UK Indymedia, 2008). It envisions itself in 'Indymedia: Precursors and

Birth' as a 'true alternative to the corporate's network—a people's network' (233). Long-term goals of Indymedia, as declared in its 'Principles of Unity' online, are a world where all people are free and equal, where all resources are equally shared, and where 'no hierarchies or authority' exists, specifically not those based on race, class, gender, age, or sexual orientation. To reach such goals, which clearly show that the project engages genuinely in the pursuit of justice, Indymedia is committed to open software and non-institutionalisation. It also fosters human rights and 'direct participative democracy,' and takes a strong left-wing anti-capitalist position (Pittsburgh Indymedia, 2007; Indymedia FAQ, 2008). For instance, 'Indymedia: don't hate the media, be the media' hopefully declares that it wants a world of 'communication without commodification' (230). Indymedia views and uses new technologies as supporting the idea of non-hierarchy and alliance. David Hudson even calls Indymedia in *OpenMute* an 'international force of gandhis,' capable of stopping war (1).[14] American academic-activist DeeDee Halleck says in 'Gathering Storm: The Open Cyber Forum of Indymedia' that with this new form of activism, 'the revolution is . . . digitised and streamed' (2).

Over the several years of its existence, however, Indymedia has worked through a major number of crises that by and large revolve around how this reach for equality and freedom was to be practiced in the project groups themselves, as well as through the online open-posting format. Tensions between those who wanted Indymedia to be the ultimate free-speech portal, and others who believed censorship of unwanted postings is required, have led to the breakdown of various local Indymedia groups. These crises, as I suggested earlier, appear to be structural to Indymedia, and have involved a constant and precarious repositioning and reproduction of parameters around what kind of postings and alliances Indymedia desires.[15] The aporia that lies at the base of Indymedia's sympathetic call for justice appears as a constant crisis of *legitimisation*, and the decisions made in light of these crises push it forward—a (re)production (and acceleration) that in turn dissimulates this aporia. In many Indymedia texts, just like in Lovink's work, new technologies are indeed constantly re-envisioned as the tools that will eventually help overcome this crisis—the re-politicisation of technologies that, as I discussed by way of Dean's work, lies at the heart of the problem. As I will show later on, this quest for justice through new technologies is informed by a speed-elitist fantasy of establishing ultimate control. This expresses itself as a call for freedom, connectivity, mobility, and 'fun.'

A good example of this call for freedom as fun for the privileged is Matthew Arnison's 'Open publishing is the same as free software,' one of the foundational Indymedia manifestos. Arnison says that open publishing, or the idea that a reader can contribute his own story on a news website, equals free software because both these principles adhere to the idea of 'freedom.' So freedom in general, which Arnison problematically translates into the freedom for 'free beer' and to creatively 'produce anything awe-inspiring [and] enjoyable,' boils down to 'software freedom, a software liberation movement' (1). His final conclusion is thus that 'information wants to be free' and he attacks corporations like Microsoft for 'keeping software closed' (2). He goes on to claim that the Internet is radically different from the previous media, because instead of the disconnection and alienation that large media corporations like Microsoft and CNN foster, on the Internet 'information flows . . . forming a much more balanced web' (2). In much the same way, activist Aditya Nigam says enthusiastically in 'The Old Left in a New World' about Indymedia that 'One of the most striking aspects of this movement is its extremely fluid and mobile character, powered through the new communication technologies, such that it is able to move from one location to another in almost immaterial form' (4). However, far from Microsoft being activist open-source software's opposite, Arnison's narrative of freedom is eerily in line with Microsoft's ideals of friction-free capitalism without noise, in which information needs to flow incessantly and instantaneously. Nigam's metaphor of fluidity and mobility is also remarkably similar to the actual immediate movements of flash capital and the free mobility of those who are empowered by it. Such a form of capitalism hardly allows for 'a more balanced web'—on the contrary, Arnison's rhetoric covertly serves to enhance the exclusionary workings of the new technologies by 'buying into' the discourse of the need for speed and 'free flow of information.'

It may therefore come as no surprise that Indymedia came into existence as the 'bastard son' of 'Seattle, home of Microsoft,' as a volunteer in *IMC—A New Model* put it (10). But far from the supposedly subversive connotations that the term 'bastard' may carry, one could similarly claim that Indymedia is equally its 'son.' In fact, the term 'bastard son' is an apt metaphor for how Indymedia's work of justice cannot be separated from the (unintentional) violence it does through its complicity in speed. Arnison, for instance, compares the desire to build something awe-inspiring and enjoyable to the building of the pyramids, and contends that building these required a lot of slave labour (3). But he goes on to say that 'We've evolved as a species . . . Forget the pyramids. Bypass world domination' (4), brushing aside the opportunity for an analysis of the contemporary slave labour required to sustain his desires for 'freedom' by simply claiming that humanity has 'evolved.' One may think here of the harsh labour conditions in Mexican maquiladoras and Asian electronics sweatshops as modern slave labour, and of how these conditions relate to the intensification of global and local inequalities in terms of gender and race. What is more, it is exactly these technologies that allow him as well as other well-meaning new-media volunteers to keep those 'slaves' just conveniently out of sight. For him, then, the utopia of '[o]pen publishing [that] just might help us use those wires to save the planet' (4) remains alive since he makes no connection at all as to how the materiality of those 'wires' relates to 'world domination' and the 'mass extinction of species' he is rightly concerned about in an earlier paragraph.

This naivety about neo-liberal capitalism repeatedly dominates discussions on Indymedia lists, and I also participated in this when working for Indymedia. These discussions are unaware of this form of capitalism as the generator of those new technologies of representation and connection that allow the speed-elite to project their fantasies of fun and freedom *as if* they were anti-corporate. Indymedia volunteers and intellectual proponents, for instance, instantly booed the intriguing suggestion at a Next Five Minutes event in 2003 that Indymedia works like a brand name. In another example several years ago, Indymedia volunteers in Western Europe expressed their anti-corporate disgust over an American Indymedia collective buying an apartment in which to put their equipment, until one volunteer rightly reminded them that the Dutch website runs on the wires of an Amsterdam Internet provider that is part of KPNQWest—the then largest corporate Internet conglomerate and backbone provider in Europe. The volunteer also pointed out that the organisation that hosts the Indymedia editing server is sponsored by the Dutch state. And all this takes place while the Dutch website professes that Indymedia is an 'independent communication channel, unlike corporate or state-run media.'

Like Arnison, early Indymedia programmer and activist Evan Henshaw-Plath on the Mediapolitics list also problematically equates the idea of open publishing with open software in many of his writings. This is apparent in the answers from Henshaw-Plath which he posted online as part of an interview by someone from *Online Journalism Review*. His responses are particularly interesting because he seems quite aware of the neo-liberal nature of the new media technologies Indymedia is implicated in. He notices, for instance, that the open-publishing idea of disseminating authority and power from the website editor to the readers sounds 'like a phrase pulled out of the dot-com go-go days' (3), as it is the lure of 'interactivity' that allows readers to have a (false) fantasy of control over information and technology in general—a fantasy that is nonetheless essential for a left-wing humanist politics. This notion of (inter)activity as straightforwardly liberatory nonetheless curiously informs the rest of Henshaw-Plath's responses and other Indymedia narratives. We could relate this notion to the consumer discourse of the speed-elite through the hegemony of Eucken's politically energised person I mentioned in Chapter 1: more (inter)activity equals more capital flows. Equating Indymedia directly with Bey's idea of the TAZ, Henshaw-Plath in turn aptly describes the expansion of Indymedia as due to the fact that

> There is a frenetic pace which draws people in. . . . There is a feeling that this is where the action is. A *mix of revolutionary protests and dot-com like caffeine fuelled energy of technology*. More than anything else, *this energy* is what's driven the rapid growth of the Indymedia network. I've heard it be described as it feeling like you're walking in to a big collective brain. Everything pulsing this way and that, information

rushing around, spreading out and taking in information. It's a high tech temporary autonomous zone. (2, italics mine)

This lucid report on the energy that drives Indymedia demonstrates that the ideas of political activism and revolution seem to agree very well with the idea of dot-com technology and networking, and infuses left-wing activism with a proper amount of 'frenzy'—the hallmark of speed-elitism. Henshaw-Plath indeed depicts the intensification of humanism and its collusion with neo-liberal acceleration in full colours. The desires that draw people like me into Indymedia are, although well-meant, by no means autonomous or subversive: instead, they are effects of the (empowering) neo-liberal power structures of the speed-elite, made possible by a global militarisation. In this light, Henshaw-Plath's numerous allusions of 'giving the power to the people' through Indymedia says nothing about how revolutionary such an endeavour is and does not explain at all which people are able to use it most. Moreover, he romantically bestows the *faculty* of liberation on an 'oppressed people' when he says that

> I see my task as building technological systems where *people* can exert power through egalitarian systems that will reproduce horizontal and cooperative social relations and institutions. (6)

This homogenisation of 'people' in general as 'the' marginalized, which dangerously confuses various potentially oppositional and uneven struggles under the umbrella of techno-inspired alter-globalism, returns also in Indymedia's rhetoric of 'the Struggle' (UK Indymedia, 2007). This confusion is dangerous because it accelerates a highly militarised and increasingly unstable technocratic politics. One Indymedia volunteer describes his experiences in the alter-globalist compendium *we are everywhere* with 'The room was buzzing with activity, everybody seemed to know what they were doing' (Indymedia 2003, 231), which sounds very much like the atmosphere at the Amsterdam stock exchange or at a military headquarters during wartime. Like Henshaw-Plath's description of Indymedia as a 'brain buzzing with activity,' it appears that such technologies of speed and the neo-liberal context they are enmeshed with *invoke* strong desires of political engagement and connection—these are not some inherent quality of 'people.' Moreover, the sense of buzz and of being on the frontier of activity and technology described by this activist only *seemingly* unites all volunteers in a single goal. These technologies thus powerfully allow a playing out of such desires of virtualisation and a fantasy of connecting with the other. Allow me to stress here once more the utter direness of the situation for alter-globalist activism when the new technological arrangements *transform* acting responsibly into responsibility's own withdrawal.

This emphasis on interactivity and openness, as well as the fantasy of decentralisation and freedom through the new technologies, is a myth that firmly ties in with capitalist conditions of production and consumption through exactly these technologies and their liberatory discourses. Furthermore, the notions of interactivity and openness suggest again a humanist myth that imagines subjectivity as somehow liberating itself by mastering its technologies. This is because the notion of interactivity erroneously suggests that humans and machines are discreet entities, and that new interactive technologies allow for more human agency. Instead, though, human agency appears to be dwindling rapidly. The claim that Indymedia is revolutionary, counter-corporate, and alter-globalist in Henshaw-Plath's narrative paradoxically reproduces those globalising powers it seeks to overcome. This is because it reinstalls the belief in political activity, speed, and the idea of progress that precisely inform a neo-liberalism inspired by an Eucken-like humanism. Indeed, at the start of the interview Henshaw-Plath says, 'I gave up my apartment and quit my corporate job so I could travel around and provide tech support for the revolution' (1). But all the while Henshaw-Plath draws no connection between his privileged ability to quit his job and travel around freely and the rhetoric and infrastructure of speed which allow him to do so. He is therefore effectively, although probably inadvertently, making a case first and foremost for his own and the speed-elite's upward mobility.

In light of such neo-liberal reproduction through a constant compulsion for legitimisation—which Indymedia performs in its responsible acting out of the humanist call for justice—it is interesting to note how the project has changed since its creation on Lovink's, Bey's, and Arnison's speed-elitist principles. Indymedia in its 'Principles of Unity' translates their visions of 'free flow' and 'open spaces' as 'open exchange of and open access to information are a prerequisite to the building of a more free and just society' (2). The main source of heated disagreement and perplexity among Indymedia volunteers revolves around how to deal with the increasing number of unwanted fascist, sexist, racist, or homophobic postings, which obviously do not agree with Indymedia's humanist quest for eliminating inequalities. From the start, *The IMC—A New Model* aporetically declared that Indymedia wants to become more 'accessible, open and democratic' (13) while simultaneously aspiring to a model where 'most local sites are now closely monitored, with articles ranked . . . to reinforce global diversity and unity' (14).

The most striking example of how deep this crisis of contradiction runs in Indymedia was the provisional closure of Indymedia-Switzerland in 2002 due to disputes about how to handle the massive flooding of anti-Semitic and right-wing postings. The Dutch Indymedia, of which I was part, suffered from similar troubles, which resulted in an official warning letter from the Dutch Organization against Discrimination on the Internet (MDI) demanding a complete halt to any remotely racist postings on the website (Netherlands Indymedia, 2002). The increasing number of unwanted postings on the Indymedia websites has over the years resulted in animated discussion and eventually in a change of editorial policy regarding the website. In the early stages of Indymedia, the website consisted of two columns on the front page: one column, called the 'newswire,' was completely open for anybody to post messages on, and messages would appear instantaneously. The other column, usually slightly larger on the left of the main page, would represent those messages that were selected by the editorial board. Gradually, this dual newswire system disappeared from most Indymedia websites to make space for a triple or even quadruple system (see, for instance, Pittsburgh Indymedia, 2007; Netherlands Indymedia 2008)—hoping that more software layers would solve the issue. One main column would contain the editorial summaries of messages that were perceived as important and valuable, while the column on the right would contain those open postings that were approved for reading. One click away from the main page would be a column with all open postings except the discriminatory ones, the latter of which could only be found more clicks away in a trash column or web area completely closed off from public view. This compromise between being an open channel and moderating the website closely did not and still does not go without a fight; when New York IMC adopted a moderation policy in 2003, heartfelt cries about the evil of censorship abounded (NYC Indymedia, 2003). It is striking how these structural crises that inhabit the Indymedia project are constantly sought to be solved through software or hardware adaptation, as if the next invention in open source will finally eliminate the source of such crises and make Indymedia the ultimate liberatory tool. This displays the peculiar speed-elitist faith in technological progress and the humanist outlook that grounds Indymedia, even though one may wonder how such technological solutions have made Indymedia more 'just'—at any rate, the anti-censorship groups obviously do not think so. The Indymedia concept seems already at odds with its own democratic aims.

As we saw with my reading in Chapter 1 of Derrida's point that the 'open' or 'unconditional space' is essentially made possible by neo-liberalism which renders it productive, societal inequalities get reproduced in the 'open' website and editorial Indymedia space. This explains the lack of representation of women, lower classes and ethnic minorities, or people of colour within most of Indymedia's editorial and technical areas, as well as on the level of the postings committed to feminist or anti-racist topics. This lack is despite the fact that Indymedia has always welcomed more representation and participation by marginalised groups. Indeed, Indymedia warily admits in *The IMC—A New Model* whose volunteers 'tend to represent young, white, professional class men from countries of the North' (11). The managing and programming of the Indymedia software, as Nick Couldry also remarks in 'Beyond the Hall of Mirrors,' remains a highly specialised job, also or maybe even more so because of the use of open-source software. Contrary to Arnison's conclusion that 'if someone doesn't like [the software], they can take it and change it' (1), one needs the privileges of higher education and the potential luxury of spare time to do so. Similarly, those Indymedia websites that have a rubric of feminism, anti-sexism, or anti-racism overall get few postings on these topics. Worse even, more often than not critical feminist and anti-racist postings get ridiculed online through sexist remarks and jokes.[16]

The source of this problem of continuing discrimination inside Indymedia groups lies partly with the consensus principle in Indymedia's editorial boards, which is parallel in spirit to the open-posting principle of its websites. This democratic principle of consensus, although vital for an inclusive left-wing politics, also suggests that all participants in the discussion (apart from whether the participants constitute a good representation of the variety of 'marginalised' standpoints) are on an equal footing with each other in society and in Indymedia. But although a majority-democratic process arguably establishes the 'tyranny of the majority,' the consensus process tends to represent the will of the 'biggest screamer' (as one frustrated Dutch Indymedia editor and friend put it), or those with the most time and best tools on their hands to scream. In many Indymedias, the problem of reaching consensus, and the continuing disagreement on how open or how free from unwanted postings the website should be, gets downplayed as merely a clash of characters. Over the years, the consensus principle thus has been amended by the notion of 'consensus minus one' or even 'consensus minus two,' which means that a consensus can also be reached when one or two members keep actively blocking a proposal (Los Angeles Indymedia, 2004). The policy has been changed to the extent that, even when consensus minus two fails, a majority vote will prevail. This amendment of consensus policy, which tries to diminish aggressive blocking of proposals by one or two powerful individuals, also has the effect of potentially cancelling out minority positions. More seriously, a lot of these and other decisions in Indymedia are made on email or IRC (Internet Relay Chat), which requires constant connection and speedy reaction, effectively excluding those who are slower or not connected (at that time).

In any case, the 'clash of characters' explanation and consensus-minus-two revision ignore the fact that the cause of the problem is again far more structural. A specific humanist, middle-class, highly connected, and individualist idea of the subject underlies these principles and technical revisions: a subject who can express her- or himself convincingly and coherently, and who is enabled by cultural and economic capital to use the media communication tools to his or her personal enhancement. The idea that such tensions and inequalities can be overcome is therefore what confuses Indymedia with the speed-elitist discourses and tools of freedom, connectivity, control, flexibility, liberation, and democracy.

As an inherent part of the left-wing idea of technological progress, there emerges a desire to constantly re-establish and universalise its precarious identity as 'truly allying with the oppressed.' This has driven the Indymedia project to extend its reach—in a rather missionary fashion—beyond the initial network. Arnison already mentions in his manifesto that Indymedia '*must* [make] *links* to resistance groups in poor countries . . . before [it] can call itself a people's media' (13, italics mine). Another recent instance of this desire for the margins, productively covering over the aporia of humanism by expanding the global technological network, is the call, initiated by European Indymedia volunteer Boud in 2005, to set up an Indymedia in Iran. I am giving this sympathetic call as an example not in order to vilify this engaged volunteer but because it reached a relatively large activist audience and gathered much praise. This indicates again that many activists and academics do not grasp the direness and ambiguity of the contemporary situation. It also shows well how (left-wing) politics has worryingly become a main ingredient of acceleration. In a number of emails, the European volunteer invokes a fantasy of Indymedia saving the Iranians from an upcoming military and propaganda invasion by the U.S. government. It addresses 'the' Iranians as 'fond bloggers' and claims that a subversion of U.S. propaganda in Iran will be more effective than in the case of Iraq, because many more Iranians have an Internet connection. Also, Iran is depicted to have a 'genuine, democratic process of struggles' whereas Iraq does not; so although the Iraqis were 'unable to defend themselves . . . we [Iranians and Indymedia volunteers] have the technical communication power to stop this war' (1).

This call is, in all its good intentions, stunningly naïve and optimistic about the inherently subversive powers of Indymedia and Internet communication. The emotional investment in Indymedia and its technologies is almost palpable here. Eventually, the very spread of Internet technology and the building of a networked alliance with 'the' Iranians become the essential outcome for the volunteer, when the volunteer ends with 'what's more important is for networking to happen, and for information to flow.' Whereas the volunteer usefully wants to disable the United States' propaganda efforts in Iran and help the Iranians, its own propagation of the required liberatory spread of new technologies is exactly in line with the often Western-centric reproduction of the myth of the benevolence of technocratic neo-liberal capital for the 'developing world.' The supposed non-hierarchy of Indymedia claimed by the volunteer both in its nodal technicity and its having 'no leader' (1) is then misguided. This is because it problematically dissimulates the intrinsically uneven and racially exoticised relationship between Indymedia and 'the Iranians' that such highly mediated spaces of interaction reproduce. 'The Iranians' serve as a stepping-stone to prove Indymedia's liberatory practices as universal. They also serve as objects for an alliance with the oppressed that falsely imagines Indymedia as completely outside U.S. propaganda and power. The idea of expanding open communications channels and forging alliances as a justification of 'non-hierarchy' is therefore again a dangerous illusion. The mere existence of alliance says nothing about the historical violence that belies such an alliance.

This continuing reproduction of the 'deserving marginal' in Indymedia at large over the past years is striking. It is related to the desperate upholding of the humanist utopia I mentioned before. It typically runs through a number of false oppositions, and usually finds proof of its progressiveness in any allies from the so-called global South. Its exemplary form emerges in Indymedia texts through the story of Indymedia's nascence in the Zapatistas movement. In 'Emerging Alternatives,' activist Gal Beckerman talks about how the inspiration for Indymedia came from a speech from subcomandante Marcos, who said that mainstream media only shows VIPs, whereas the 'common people only appear for a moment—when they kill someone, or when they die' (4). The alternative would therefore lie in showing 'what is really happening . . . to the people who inhabit every corner of this world.' This alternative media strategy translates in Indymedia into anti-corporate or anti-government stances, where Indymedia again portrays itself as being effectively independent from such institutions. In 'The Independent Media Center Movement,' for instance, founder Jeff Perlstein claims that Indymedia creates a 'space for civil society, free of commercial and governmental influence' (2) based on the model of the Zapatistas. This narrative of origin problematically takes the rhetoric of Zapatistas leader Marcos, as well as the Zapatistas strategies, as transparently liberatory. This is in effect a problematic romanticisation and a taking out of context of those who are then imagined to constitute an example of 'the ultimately oppressed' under globalisation—the Zapatistas. Such a romanticisation ultimately serves the vision that underlies Indymedia, in which such a strategy of 'alternative' networking and news production through the 'non-hierarchical' new technologies is supposed to be liberating for all and everyone worldwide. In line with this romanticisation, a sort of mediated disappearance-as-subversion figures in 'Indymedia: who are we?' through the claim that the Indymedia-Argentina voices consequently 'disappeared . . . [and] we discovered that others spoke' (243). This resonates also with the Zapatista catchphrase that 'nosotros no somos nosotros.'[17] But the idea that 'others speak' is a problematic denial of these Indymedia volunteers' responsibility and locality by once more taking this specific Zapatista slogan out of context. It is also a misrepresentation of their technologies as noise-free transparent media depicting the 'reality' of voices, which serves to strengthen Indymedia's fantasy of itself as authentically (re)presenting oppressed peoples.

This fantasy of Indymedia being the ultimate liberating tool is echoed by Henshaw-Plath in Beckerman's 'Emerging Alternatives.' Beckerman says that everywhere he goes, 'people' want to start an Indymedia. But a positive reception of the Indymedia format by certain people does not appreciate at all to what extent the new global conditions of possibility *compel* many people to hook up with the neo-liberal machine of acceleration that Indymedia is part of. Furthermore, it does not look at how the universalisation of its underlying humanism is complicit in this spreading force. Sheri Herndon claims in 'Modern Day Muckrakers: The Rise of the Independent

Media Center Movement' that 'empowering people to make up their minds is what Indymedia is about, and the government doesn't want you to do that' (5). But I must suggest by now that 'the government' (and definitely its ISPs) might celebrate the existence of Indymedia as proof that the United States is a 'genuine democracy' and its people so properly engaged, emancipated, and *political*, even though it may also assume it is playing with fire. In the final assessment, though, its speed-elites thrive on the increased productivity through new technologies and the spread of its neo-liberal techno-happy rhetoric, while its new technologies contain and eliminate the political efficacy of any oppositional noise and dissent.

All in all, Indymedia shows us in detail the desperate conundrum that contemporary left-wing activism finds itself in. It grounds itself in highly humanist and modernist notions of freedom, passion, resistance, liberation, and radicality, but problematically fantasises that its own passion for politics and desire for freedom exist outside the neo-liberal spaces of acceleration. It rightly demonises 'the corporate media's distortions and unwillingness to portray the truth' as the source of the oppressions under globalisation, but is itself sadly enmeshed in precisely the same structures and discourses of oppression. It also creates a flawed image of 'the people' as some homogeneously oppressed group harbouring inherent 'desires for liberation.' Such a discourse renders Internet technologies as neutral or even as simply endowing freedom and progress. The activist subject is uncritically presented as in control of the technological repercussions of its actions, which is precisely the fantasy that the hegemony of the speed-elite requires in order to manage and bank on its continuing instability and proliferation of crises. Again, and in line with Derrida's description of humanist responsibility in 'The Future of the Profession,' Indymedia confirms its heritage by internalising it, as the ideas of freedom or liberation from neo-liberal constraints reproduce those very constraints. And they reproduce these, it seems, in an ever-accelerating manner.

ACADEMIC OPTIMISM AND INDYMEDIA ACTIVISM

Although academic studies of Indymedia are numerous, there are several works here that are worth considering for their laudable allegiance to Indymedia. Whereas all these studies have merit, I argue that they seriously limit the spirit of emancipatory activism due to falling in the trap of seeing activism as a romantic object of analysis. These studies hence implicitly mobilise the tension between action and theory, which in turn, as I explained in Chapter 1, feeds acceleration. Especially prevalent in sociological studies about Indymedia is the romantic de-contextualisation of the Zapatista struggle in Mexico as Indymedia's forebear. The Zapatista struggle has problematically come to serve as proof that Indymedia—and indeed any other new communications-network-inspired activism—is liberatory or subversive. A good example of this is the work of academic scholar and Indymedia activist Jeffrey Juris, who regularly draws from the work of autonomist Harry Cleaver.[18] Juris is fascinating because his work exemplifies the activist and academic sensation of being on the forefront of social change. He inhabits the activist spirit while remaining blind to its moorings in exclusionary acceleration, just as I myself have in the past. In 'Indymedia: From Counter-Information to Informational Utopics,' Juris unabashedly celebrates the existence of Indymedia by arguing that it inherited its subversive and anti-capitalist logic from the Zapatistas. Juris, however, does not make clear how this genealogy came about; he simply says that the Zapatistas were 'anti-state' and 'anti-corporate,' and that they used the Internet to disseminate their stories and organise events (5, 6). He then conveniently deduces that this use of the Internet is 'un-hierarchical.' He continues this success story by claiming that the Internet 'does not simply provide the technological infrastructure of social movements; its reticulate structure reinforces their organizational logic' (9), and that therefore 'decentralized networks like Indymedia facilitate instantaneous communication, collaboration, coordination and action (C3A)' (10). But while he seeks to have this narrative prove Indymedia's anti-capitalism, such rhetoric is instead completely in line with the terms of informational capitalism's C3I[19]: speed of information, 'control through decentralisation' (9), 'self-regulation' (15), and 'trans-nationality' (21). Juris, like Bey and Lovink, invents a narrative of superseding neo-liberal capitalism ('new' technologies, 'challenging' corporations, 'autonomous' elements, 'radical' politics, 'horizontal' structures) by naturalising speed-elitist discourse—a technologically utopian narrative that he repeats in his later 'The New Digital Media and Activist Networking within Anti-Corporate Globalization Movements' as well as his *Networking Futures*, which even concludes that new media activism is a 'laboratory' of an emerging democratic politics that will lead us to an 'informational utopics' (267). This blatant naturalisation of speed-elitism takes place because Juris is oblivious to his activities in terms of circulation and production, both of his activism and his scholarly technique of participatory observation. This rhetorical trick is in fact often used in social-science research, and consists in the pretence of neutrally describing an object of research (in this case, Indymedia) from within, as if the politics of academia is unrelated to the social hierarchies that also constitute Indymedia. Instead, as I argued in Chapter 1, there exists a strong relationship between theoretical and social hierarchies. Juris's pretence to objectivity therefore results in a legitimisation of academia and its gatekeeping procedures through the romanticisation of activisms and new technologies as liberatory even if it seeks to counter gatekeeping procedures.

Dorothy Kidd's work forms another example of how certain academic theories are implicated in the hegemonic tactics of speed by depicting Indymedia as totally and genuinely liberatory. Kidd enthusiastically discusses the Indymedia project in 'Indymedia.org: A New Communications

Commons' as one of the new public spaces that emerged because of the Internet. She depicts the story of Indymedia mostly in terms of success and of increasing progress of visibility against corporate media. She claims Indymedia is based on a non-hierarchical structure (60) and argues that it 'helped to break down, if not eliminate, some of the territorial divisions' between various media activists worldwide (61). The problem with Kidd's discussion is firstly that it does not problematise at all the notions of 'the commons' or 'public space' that Indymedia supposedly enhances. Also, it does not qualify the colonialist spreading of these ideas and their tools as historically specific. Secondly, as a result of this strategy, Kidd re-creates the grand North American story of the emergence, application, and spread of the new technologies as a mostly positive or at best neutral affair. One typical effect of this American romantic falsification is that Kidd describes the origins and the basic faculties of the Internet as—you guessed it—fundamentally good and open to all. According to her, the Internet stems from some altruist and democratic common effort on the side of academia, the U.S. military (!), and several early hacktivists, only to be taken over gradually by the bad boys of corporate enterprises and copyright protectors (56). Kidd uses this demonisation of today's corporatisation to invoke nostalgia for the early days of the Internet and Internet research. But this nostalgia ignores that it was exactly the American and European universities, together with some early cyber-activist groups and military institutions and corporations, which created the very technologies that make current neo-liberal capitalism and corporatisation possible. Kidd obscures through this simple opposition the overt complicity of academia, activists, corporate, and state powers in each other's projects. It is this nostalgia and the strategic forgetting of the violent history of the implications and implementations of the new technologies that 'information should be free' groups like Indymedia incessantly invoke. Kidd acknowledges, for instance, that 'the IMC would not have been possible without the convergence of new levels of social movement and new technology. . . . the IMC could overcome the limited space and distribution problems . . . the Internet enabled a quantum leap . . . the reach is potentially so much further' (49, 62). But while this statement is factually true, she does not complicate how Indymedia and its participants therefore become the *agents* behind the accelerating spread of new technologies and their discourses and military might under neo-liberalism.

In 'Indymedia Journalism: A Radical Way of Making, Selecting and Sharing News?' Sara Platon and Mark Deuze repeat Kidd's questionable celebration of the 'public' in different words. They define Indymedia as an 'innovation commons' because of the Internet's 'inherent democratic, chaotic, decentralised nature and freedom from official control' (337). Platon and Deuze see the premise of Indymedia as a 'fundamental critique of commercial, corporate mainstream mass media organisations' (338). Interestingly, however, they end their article with the conclusion that the experiences and dilemmas of Indymedia's editors are very close to those of mainstream media journalists' experiences. Also, they say that the mainstream media could actually see Indymedia as both a competitor and colleague (352) and they urge for a fruitful exchange of experiences, technologies, and policies between the two. The actual closeness of Indymedia's practices to those of corporate newsmakers may ring foul to those Indymedia activists who perceive their practices, as Platon and Deuze suggested at the beginning, as the complete antithesis of corporate (media) structures.

This incongruity (or deconstruction) of Deuze and Platon's arguments and the original Indymedia premises indicate to which extent the idea of activist practices as outside neo-liberal structures constitutes the main premise upon which activists empower themselves *through* these structures of acceleration. The result is again that these material and discursive structures spread and gain in force. Platon and Deuze indeed remark casually halfway through their article that 'the ideology of an open publishing network such as an IMC seems to be inherently normative' (345). This observation is at odds their earlier romantic assessment of the Internet as inherently democratic and of Indymedia as essentially non-hierarchical in nature. Platon and Deuze, however, do not delve deeper into the number of paradoxes between freedom and constraint that riddle their article, leaving a more intricate critique of Indymedia hanging in midair.

FROM TECHNOLOGY TO MOBILITY

My analyses of how Indymedia is folded into neo-liberalism show exactly that Indymedia's opposition to capitalism and corporate media is heavily implicated in the discourses and technologies of the 'fascism' (as Judith Butler would have it above) of neo-liberal capitalism it seeks to resist. What is more, Indymedia's (idea of) resistance indeed helps to replicate that 'fascism' of speed-elitism *due to* Indymedia's own democratic intentions. The appeal to truth that Indymedia purports indeed casts onto something else what essentially resides within itself. In this case, it involves a demonisation of corporate media and globalisation, even though those oppressing discourses of neo-liberal globalisation that Indymedia adheres to are precisely those which empower its users. This is not in the least to say that the corporate media have clean hands, but rather to state that Indymedia is exemplary of humanist aporia-induced acceleration.

What should worry us as left-wing activists is that Indymedia constitutes by now a successful player in the archive fever that has inspired the colonial and humanist projects, and currently inspires neo-liberal globalisation. Such fever—obsessing increasingly with technology and feeling that it is one's democratic *duty* to archive—in effect suppresses and obliterates a manifold of cultures and ways of being. Indymedia's intention of 'archiving otherness' sadly works in accordance with speed-elitism. This intention entails the dangerous *fantasy* of reaching out to the other and the withdrawal of responsibility that communication technologies are engaged in.[20] We can see that Indymedia fits just that bill. So challenging Dean once more, I conclude that politics is not foreclosed, but that politics has *intensified*. The blossoming of academic studies on Indymedia, as well as structural accidents like the September 11 attacks, prove how the ambiguous desires for democracy and freedom become magnified due to technocratic capitalism.

But to leave the analysis hanging here would focus too much on the determinable future of acceleration, and on the mere repetition within *différance*, to use Derrida's helpful neologism. The above quote from *The IMC—A New Model,* with which I started the Indymedia analysis, interestingly begins by mentioning that it is 'love for people' that drives the Indymedia project. This is laudable; but as I argued in Chapter 1, despite the benevolent connotation that the term 'love' in the quote is supposed to invoke, love is not univocally benevolent. Instead, the workings of love must necessarily involve a self-love or egotism—an assertion of in this case its speed-elitist self. This egotism nonetheless remains at base impossible to distinguish from its altruism, since it also involves some kind of invitation of something else. It is this non-neutral affirmation of the speed-elitist self that is heavily implicated in the discourses of speed, but this then also means that Indymedia's love for justice is open for critical appropriations beyond its intention—like the one I have instigated here. Such a similarity in our declarations of justice, which remains in excess of my and Indymedia activism, therefore opens up a critical engagement with one of the oppositions that run through the mixing of post-structuralism and activism. Perhaps we could call this excess their *spirit*. As such, it is not set in stone where all these invitations may lead.

In any case, we can conclude from the analyses in this chapter that new and social media activisms are quite productive—in the capitalist and democratic sense of the word—during their trajectories towards a certain humanist utopia. This is also because they are largely unaware of the repetitions of acceleration that underlie their imaginations. Whereas such complicity is indeed necessary for contemporary political action and thought, it supplies, I suggest, primarily those margins that were already upwardly mobile, as well as the speed-elite itself. The aim of mapping out such complicities of new media activism, as I have done here, is not eventually to claim that a politics or an activism is possible that may transcend such complicities, and that may become liberating for all. Such a claim would reproduce those myths of liberation it seeks to critique. Instead, the very *impossibility of non-complicity* points to the conundrum that nowadays critiquing or resisting neo-liberal power involves the use and reproduction of its concepts and tools. This conundrum operates on the level of new-media activist protests, but also on the level of this book and its entanglements with certain institutions that facilitate late-capitalist production. It calls forward and is the result of the continuing desire to identify with and uphold a narrative of emancipatory progress. If we, as alter-globalist academics and activists, so desperately want Indymedia to be liberatory and at the same time want change only as long as we can keep our computers and our mobility, as Dean lucidly remarked (63), then those avenues to express our desires must be an effect of exactly the reciprocal complicity of the discourses of liberation, being political, and speed. If the survival of certain groups and individuals depends on the abandonment of 'old' ways of life and on their insertion into well-meaning but complicit practices in the face of speed like Indymedia, then the situation indeed looks grim and complex in the extreme.

But this book cannot wash its hands in innocence and simply make a Luddite call to abandon all technologies of complicity. After all, I mentioned in the previous chapter that we cannot *not* commit when we speak in the name of justice. Put differently, to denounce media politics as such would be profoundly *insincere*. Demonising new technologies would not appreciate the tools and techniques that made critical readings and engagements possible in the first place, and can therefore not be the antidote to the celebratory tone prevalent in Juris's and Kidd's studies. What is required is a closer look at the constitutive imaginations that facilitate and surround these narratives, so as to slowly and thoughtfully double the affirmations that underlie them. Also, we would need to bring the analysis closer to its own politics—without wanting to get too self-absorbed—by acknowledging the deconstruction of this book.

I would therefore like to continue into another set of fantasies that the three alter-globalist activisms and much current academic theory in the humanities and social sciences typically engage in vis-à-vis globalisation. These fantasies entail the problematic universalisation of 'the struggle' and the recent romanticisation of the migrant as the ideal speed metaphor for *crossing borders*.

3 The Migrant
The Speed-Elite's Daydream of Radical Alterity

> Throughout the ontological terrain of globalisation the most wretched of the earth becomes the most powerful being, because its new nomad singularity is the most creative force and the omnilateral movement of its desire is itself the coming liberation.
>
> Michael Hardt and Antonio Negri, *Empire* (363, 2000).

> Let us then, for the moment at least, arrest the understandable need to fix and diagnose the identity of the most deserving marginal. Let us also suspend the mood of self-congratulation as saviours of marginality.
>
> Gayatri Chakravorty Spivak,
> 'Marginality in the Teaching Machine' (61, 1993).

THE RISE OF A METAPHOR IN RADICAL THOUGHT

As I explained in the previous chapter, the complicities of new media activism in acceleration run through various hallucinations of radical alterity, like the romanticisation and objectification of 'the' Zapatistas, 'the' Iranians, or even 'the' people. These romanticisations are particularly problematic because they mistakenly oppose the desires from those groups of people with 'oppressive institutions' like the corporate media, whereas oftentimes such desires are *effects* of such powerful arrangements. The opposing of desires from 'the' margins versus neo-liberalism homogenises groups, and disregards internally divisive issues of class, gender, and race. It also dissimulates the entanglements of its own discourse of resistance in acceleration. The general homogenisation of the folks which I discussed in Chapter 2 notwithstanding, I suggest in this chapter that there exists under speed-politics one particularly popular romanticisation: that of the migrant. An analysis of this contemporary obsession with the migrant fruitfully complicates alter-globalism as well as this book further. This is because it draws us closer to the issues of the mutual relatedness and complicities of contemporary alter-globalist activism and theorisation under neo-liberal capitalism, which occur as the effect of the dominant discourses of trans-national mobility, resistance, and new media as some kind of 'open' or 'unconditional' space. The current romanticisation of 'the migrant' is also in many ways an updated version of the techno-happy celebrations of the hybrid and the cyborg, which was and still is quite pervasive in various academic circles during the globalisation of computer networks in the 1990s. The persistence of such metaphors in activist and intellectual work points to an amplification of the supposed benevolence of the discourses and (techno-logically endowed) potentials to cross borders, which are both crucial to the speed-elite.

The lived conditions of refugees and migrants gained quick ground as a legitimate source of politicised resistance and research in various European and Australian activist and intellectual circles. Activist groups like Kein Mensch ist Illegal, AG3F (Anti-Racist Group for Free Flooding), Autonoom Centrum and the No-Border network in Europe,[1] as well as, for instance, xborder, BaxterWatch, and Woomera2002 in Australia,[2] have prolifer-ated. This proliferation went together with an increased focus by European Union (EU) and International Office of Migration (IOM) policymakers on what these policymakers tend to call 'effectively containing the migrant issue.' Simultaneously, a shift towards theoretical paradigms focusing on migration and refugee issues is on the increase in Western, and especially European, social sciences and humanities research. Since 1995 there has been a particularly huge increase in organisations, departments, and insti-tutions (like the European Research Centre on Migration and Ethnic Rela-tions) that deal with the policing, critiquing of policing, and researching of migratory flows in the European Union. The number of studies worldwide on migration issues more than tripled in this period.[3]

This upsurge in focusing on migrant issues, I argue, is symptomatic of certain pervasive desires and fears in the information age, and has caused the image of the migrant to 'travel' through left-wing academic and activ-ist circles in peculiar ways. The large conference on radical Italian thought in Sydney in September 2004 is a good example of the obsession with the migrant in academia and activism in Europe and Australia. It tellingly had as its main theme 'the multitude, refugees, and globalisation,' and many panels narrated the supposed revolutionary characteristic of cross-border practices. Especially many Italian thinkers currently theorise 'the' migrant in relation to capitalist subversion. For sure, this obsession is not without its critics. In 'Border Camps: The New "Sexy" Thing?' Wayne Foster humor-ously remarks that no-border activism is the 'next big single issue style campaign'[4] which will 'save a few professional activists from redundancy' (1). He keenly notes that such activism, heavily invested in new media tech-nologies as it often is, seems to somehow fulfil 'our desire for the spectacle of resistance' so that 'we can feel we are resisting, say we are resisting' (2). I think Foster has a great point here. So while I am aware that these activists are earnestly concerned about the agonies of refugees, I nonetheless want to extend Foster's weariness. My questions for this chapter are therefore: what underlies this increasing interest of Italian thought and alter-globalist activ-ism in the migrant or refugee? What are the complicities of the spectacle of resistance and its technological and societal underpinnings that Foster claims Italian thought and its migrant activism might aspire to?

In order to understand the peculiarities at work in migrant activism, it is pertinent to put Italian thought in its historical context. Radical Italian thought emerged out of the *operaismo* ('workerism') in northern Italy of the 1960s and 1970s, when large numbers of factory workers clashed with the Italian industrial and governmental authorities, demanding better working conditions and payment. To back up these workers' struggles, many local intellectuals sought to validate these struggles through rewriting Marxist theory. Among these intellectuals were Franco Berardi, Paolo Virno, and Antonio Negri, who started as a legal practitioner. These intellectuals assumed that radical subversive potential resided in the 'desires and subjectivities' of these workers, and they criticised the workers' unions for dampening this potential. The fertile though at times antagonistic collaboration between these intellectuals and workers became known as the *autonomia* ('autonomous') movement.[5] *Autonomia* struggles, however, became more and more violent during the 1970s, and reached a breaking point when Italian authorities decided to crack down on the aggression using extremely violent measures. Many women and feminists in the movement also started turning their backs on the machismo and misogyny within the movement. All this led to a mass abandonment of *autonomia* in the late 70s by many activists.[6]

Contemporary radical Italian thought builds largely on this heritage. It quickly gained in popularity when the *autonomia* type of Italian activist thought was revived almost twenty years later, and started bleeding over into various alter-globalist and anti-capitalist praxes around the world, especially into new media activism. The term 'radical Italian thought' today generally refers to any theorist who bases his or her writings and politics on the idea, which took root in the *autonomia* movement of the 1960s, that the practices of the oppressed worker are intrinsically subversive. I will use the term 'radical Italian thought' here as a shorthand to refer to a particular present-day subgroup of Italian and non-Italian thinkers, who have updated *autonomia* by theorising the intrinsic sedition of those 'classes' who cross borders and use new technologies. Other important radical Italian intellectuals like Antonio Gramsci, Paolo Virno, Giorgio Agamben, and Franco Berardi will only be discussed parenthetically—there where their ideas are relevant to such border-crossing arguments. The fact that the migrant has come to play a central role in this new Italian imagination makes sense especially because migrant workers from the impoverished south of Italy played a major part in the factory strikes instigated by the *autonomia* movements in northern Italy during the 1960s and 1970s.[7] But the question is very much how generalisable this migrant experience is.

Paolo Virno and Michael Hardt's 1996 book entitled *Radical Thought in Italy: A Potential Politics* (often wrongly referred to as *Radical Italian Thought*) and Michael Hardt and Antonio Negri's *Empire* are famous exponents of earlier *autonomia*. These books became major favourites in many Western academic and activist circles, and facilitated alter-globalist struggles with a rich and imaginative theoretical foundation. In 'From the Italian Laboratory of the 1970s to the Global Laboratory of a Politics Opposed to Forms of War,' Ida Dominijanni suggests that the recent interest in Italian thought also marks a shift away from the French thought of Deleuze, Derrida, and Foucault. Agamben, for instance, is portrayed as the contemporary Italian version of Deleuze, and is categorised as a radical Italian thinker, although he bears little resemblance to *autonomia*. Dominijanni also argues that this shift has been made possible by 'the explosion of the political potentiality of the Internet and media-activism' (2), and some free-software activists indeed trace their roots back to Virno and Hardt's famous book.[8] My analysis of new media activism in the previous chapter should then already make us wary of the claim to sedition in radical Italian thought.

To analyse radical Italian thought as an exemplary exponent of alter-globalist activism allows me therefore to explore more closely what romantic recuperations are available under neo-liberal globalisation, and how these may be complicit in the quest for speed. As the grandiose quote from *Empire* above shows, this quest for speed seems to invoke a fantasy of liberation that is reminiscent of an almost Christian theology about 'the wretched of the earth,' and inserts the latter into a highly networked ('nomad' and 'omnilateral') imagination of creativity and change. The recurring theme of autonomy, and the recuperation of desire and subjectivity from 'the margins' as automatically subversive, are especially dubious in this light. This is because it suggests a strengthening of an imagination of autonomy that refuses to engage with its underlying conditions of possibility. This intensification also implies a possible repetition of the misogyny of *autonomia* and an erasure of the antagonisms between the workers and the intellectuals from its collective memory. Radical Italian thought consequently allows for a thorough exploration of the relationship between alter-globalist activism and the increase of gendered, raced, and classed global disparities.

Moreover, we can identify in the strands of radical Italian thought that seek to incorporate migrant issues within their conceptual framework of alter-globalist struggles the birth of yet another hybrid praxis. Radical thought resides on the borders of the academic humanities and activist or alter-globalist knowledge construction. It is therefore important to keep these Italian thinkers under close observation, because of their close ties to and ongoing influence on academic and alter-globalist activisms, like the European and World Social Forums. In this sense, radical Italian thought joins the more than productive crossing of borders on two levels—between theorisation and activism, as well as across national borders. It is this privileged practice of crossing-over that seeks to legitimise itself by imagining the migrant as a border-crossing hero. A critique of the migrant in Italian thought is therefore urgent, even though I acknowledge that most activist and intellectual endeavours around migration, like the No-Borders campaign or radical Italian thought, are set up with the sympathetic intention of combating the racist and xenophobic EU or IOM policies. This intention is surely valid and valuable—EU and IOM policies, after all, enforce the falsehood that migration from certain countries and groups is a 'threat' in need of containment. These policies constitute the migrant or refugee as a mere object or problem, and falsely naturalise historically contingent borders and identities. However, the no-border activisms and Italian philosophies are *also* complicit in the ongoing fortification of the EU and partly of the West, as well as of the speed-elite's subsequent worldwide hegemonic spread through neo-liberal discourses and technologies, of which the technology of the nation as a sovereign institution is only one. Many radical Italian writings, through a metaphorisation of the migrant or refugee, supplement the alter-globalisation movement in effectively reproducing the speed-elitist fantasy of the humanist subject as the ultimate centre for social change, just as much as those despised EU policies do. So despite—or maybe, rather, *because of*—the seemingly altruistic and resistant intentions of the incorporation of the migrant within activism and activist thought, this incorporation is extremely self-centred and self-loving.

As I hinted at in Chapter 1, any activist or theoretical response to hegemonies that thinks of itself as a total denunciation of 'old' power today irresponsibly repeats the very structures it seeks to abolish. The humanist idea of resistance, which mystifies resistance as authentic to the human and as outside neo-liberalism, forgets that resistance today is almost entirely inscribed in the logic of speed. It is the ultimately fallacious notion of resistance that returns in these radical Italian texts. Such *hyper*-modernism as the dominant function of post-modernism and its allegiance to new technologies, as I discussed in Chapter 1, is what Borgmann analyses as a condition that shares an unreserved modernist allegiance to technology, but that differs from modernism in giving technology a design that works on many levels. New technologies in this era not only symbolise the idea of progress, and thereby uphold the ideology of overcoming all ideologies, but also increasingly allow for the *illusion* of progress by deferring or dissimulating its negative effects. Acceleration is key to such dissimulation. It is for this reason that Paul Virilio remarks in the interview 'From Modernism to Hypermodernism and Beyond' that 'we are not out of modernity, by far' (26). The history of acceleration that started with modernity and its technologies is still very much continuing and even intensifying. Virilio rather cryptically calls technocratic societies 'cinematic societies,' because they are obsessed with movement, and thus by extension with the acceleration of movement. This does not only mean that distances get shorter in terms of time, but that there is also a 'shortening' of 'the relation to reality' (27). I argue that Virilio here points to a symptom of speed-elitism similar to the withdrawal of responsibility that new technologies endow through *simulating* a reaching out to 'real' others. This means that the terms of alliance and solidarity—a false embrace of differences—that the Italian thinkers and activists portray with 'the' migrant or refugee will reside precisely in an implicit *extension of self-indulgence* and self-centredness by celebrating new technologies as progressive.

HYPER-MODERNISM, THE SPEED-ELITE, AND ITS NARRATIVE OF REDEMPTION

I outlined in Chapter 1 how the reproduction of the discourses and technologies of the speed-elite generally presents itself in alter-globalist activism. The 'double affirmation,' which shows at what point activisms deconstruct, allows us to discern one activist strategy that is increasingly pervasive under speed-elitism. It consists of the mobilisation of what I call an 'ideal other' in order to justify that activism's main outlook and aim. This mobilisation concerns a growing impulse to encapsulate or archive this other in an activist schema by means of a projection of the activist self onto this other, thereby simulating the authenticity of the emancipatory desire. Such a projection is in itself of course nothing new—feminist, anti-racist, and psychoanalytic theorists have argued for decades that modern subject formation works through mirroring. In 'Marginality in the Teaching Machine,' Gayatri Spivak, for instance, outlines how the revalidation of the West and the fantasy of the autonomous agent as the proper centre for evolution and action (whether capitalist or liberatory) rely on a constant and precarious reproduction of marginality. She exemplifies this reproduction of marginality by pointing out how her own upward mobility was produced through a Eurocentric romanticisation of herself in academic circles as an 'authentic' Indian voice. In short, her position of an 'Indian' speaking from 'the non-West' has provided her with a voice and a career, but this subjugation is also implicated in the material, discursive, and technological violence from the West onto the non-West. Any claim to authentic marginality can therefore be understood as a *commitment* to an imperialist subjugation that oppresses many other people. The upwardly mobile 'marginalised' become the *agents* of economic globalisation.[9] Activisms and theories that rely on the idea of the 'objective reality' that 'the margins' provide, profess to the hegemony that actually assigns this marginality.

The identification of 'the' (voice from the) margin, like 'the oppressed' or 'the Third World' in much alter-globalist activism, taps into an endemic aspiration to extend the humanist belief system that grounds speed-elitism. Such 'margins' then uphold the phantasm of the universal applicability of the humanist subject and its technologies. This is not to say that naming that margin cannot be empowering or productive—on the contrary, it is highly productive and empowering, but in a *very specific way* and within a very specific frame of thought and production. This also means that, while Spivak's assessment is overall an excellent one in drawing out the basic logic behind colonialism, I do disagree with her assessment of *what today constitutes the centre*—in other words, what the region or social group benefits most from this romanticisation. I argue that this centre is today no longer 'the West' but has shifted towards a much more technologically informed exaltation of speed in the service of global elites that inhabit many non-Western parts of the world. This specificity of empowerment and production through acceleration in turn unintentionally re-enforces structural local and global inequalities—especially those of class—and globalises the current ideological grounds of neo-liberalism, namely democracy, humanism, technophilia, and freedom, rooting out the many other ways of being in the world. So whereas 'the West' functions increasingly as a *sign* of hegemony, its mobilisation engenders a worldwide speed-elitism. Therefore, the possibility of and at times even compulsive desire for *connections* under mediated and accelerated capitalism have given the old colonising enterprise a new and perhaps more vicious impulse *because* it claims to overcome racism and colonialism. This is again the extreme paradox in which the humanist aporia has propelled us today. We will see later on how this *double* neo-colonialist romanticisation reproduces itself discursively not only through more obviously homogenising phrases such as 'the people' and 'our desires,' but especially through popular 'radical' terms like 'the multitude' in much activist thinking and practice.

This paradox shows itself in how neo-liberal capitalism, and its practices and ideas of acquiring freedom and emancipation, is today so intimately intertwined with the notion of technological progress that the very logic of acceleration directly exacerbates the dual working of humanism. In turn, groups susceptible to upward mobility come to signify in speed-elitist activism as 'authentic inhabitants of the margin' to the detriment of many that fail to claim such a status. The creation of alliance is thus really a means to *self*-empowerment for the speed-elitist activist, and comes about through falsely imagining that one shares the same struggles and goals as those in 'the' margin.[10] Such alliances not only reproduce the validity of the humanist utopia of the activist, but also technologically obscure the inequalities inherent in the alliance; especially since the compulsion to hook up is fundamentally unevenly spread. We saw in Chapter 2 that in new media activism this desire materialises through the erroneous activist claim that mediated spaces or channels for dialogue and collective action are 'open' or 'unconditional.' In no-border activism, the struggles from the migratory margins are imagined as authentic and subversive, and in turn become the paradigmatic fantasy of 'the' liberatory struggles of humanity at large. As I will discuss further in Chapter 4, in the course of more and more peoples becoming encapsulated in speed by way of liberatory rhetoric and techniques—or in other words, neo-liberal capitalism exhausting its prime market—activist attention shifts to animals, trees, and 'nature' as the next romantic objects.

The speed-elitist desire to identify with, snuggle up to, and even *be* the radical other is precisely at play in Italian thought and activism. So the rise of the migrant from the Third World as what Spivak calls a 'native informant' parallels the rise of an ever more sophisticated and unstable form of global capitalism.[11] This new form of capitalism entails a proliferation of military aggression concerned with rearranging re-colonisation in the name of removing barriers and borders. Spivak's theorisation, while crucial to my own interpretation of the logic of the margins, nonetheless illustrates the fundamentally schizophrenic logic that underlies the acceleration of the humanist aporia. It does this by relentlessly attempting to carve out subjective *agency* in the face of such new endemic forms of oppression. But if the idea of the subject-agent at the centre of resistance and revolution is precisely the problem, then Spivak's attempts can only seem to make arbitrary distinctions. For instance, she claims in *A Critique of Postcolonial Reason* that 'A global look at the possibility of an alternative world order must acknowledge that the migrant, although often from below, has also . . . a common interest within dominant global capital . . . there is a difference between 'get off our backs' and 'we want in' (96). But is there a difference really? Any migrant subject, especially those most disenfranchised, needs to make him- or herself today into an object or target in the face of speed in order to survive or live better. In short, she or he needs to become a *responding* and *responsible* subject who must carry forward those discourses that underlie the speed-elitist subject's culturally specific ideas of rights and freedom that Eucken's philosophy instigated. What is more, the speed-elitist subject finds redemption by way of the migrant justifying neo-liberal globalisation for him or her.[12] We can therefore expect that such a desire for humanist salvation reminiscent of Christianity is what drives many of these activists.

The mere fact that (poor) people *want* certain technologies or *want* to migrate does not mean at all that they are not being forced by circumstances. In fact, the argument that they want to migrate and that therefore technologies of travel and communication are 'good' is exactly the argument that neo-liberal globalisation uses to validate itself as benevolent. This validation continues, even though neo-liberalism inevitably runs headlong into itself when the hierarchical premises of those technologies of capitalist production, and the identity of some migrants, do not 'match.' Spivak therefore after all correctly recognises in the interview 'The Rest of the World' with Mary Zournazi that the creation of a 'general will for post-industrial finance capitalism' (179) creates a 'coercive situation that is being disguised as an invitation' (176). Indeed, 'the migrant' in much radical Italian thought works in line with masking such moments of coercion as sprouting from 'subversive free will.' Such a false localisation of authentic resistance into goals—like those of the radical Italians—shows how radical Italian thought is completely in line with neo-liberal technocratic thought. Both strands often declare that those 'poor people' just express their 'basic human right to communicate,' even though the terms and tools of communication are *imposed*, and even though the manufacture of those tools relies on the ongoing exploitation of large groups of people as well as the earth's ecosystem.

The essay 'Ready to Delete the Border' by Mexican-American migrant and border-hacker[13] Fran Illich provides a good brief example of the techno-centric nature of this confused relationship between exploitation and desire. Illich says that many people have the idea that Mexican border-hackers are against the United States and the 'new world order.' But this is not at all true, he says; instead, he and his hacking friends love all things 'American' and are actually 'pretending to be part of the American Dream' (2). Border-hackers 'simply don't believe borders should exist' and 'boundaries and borders are meant to be broken by human endeavour' (1). Illich does not explicitly make the connection between being 'pro–new world order' and these desires to delete or traverse borders; the connection is rather implicit in his text. The dissimulation of this connection nonetheless results in contradictory statements. On the one hand, he claims that the actual border remains very real throughout border-hacking, and that hacking is not 'destroying.' Yet on the other hand, he argues that 'technology and the Internet are tools that are known to break borders and erase limits' (2). One can thus conclude that the wish for the technological hacking of borders and the migration towards the United States of 'the American Dream' can only mean the *strengthening* of those borders, and that such a desire is a product of the structures that reproduce those borders. Such structures also reproduce a particularly limited view of the human as always in search of transcendence and progress. Illich's essay is nonetheless sincere in depicting the banality of his desires, agreeing that such behaviour is somehow schizo-phrenic. At the end, he even admits that 'we are confused, we accept it' (2). The reading of migrants as border-breaking heroes is hence far from trans-parent, and must instead be traced back to the same myths of transcendence through those technologies of subjectivity that erase the nation- and class-informed nature of the pushes and pulls of globalisation. Spivak remarks likewise in 'The Rest of the World' that the marginalised person under late capitalism is treated *as if* she is a subject (179). She correctly cautions that 'A sort of tear-jerking politics of the migrant destabilising the basically white-dominant state is pathetic in many ways. It's narcissistic and self-deluded. Everything is then reduced to that thing that nobody knows what it is: culture—that's where class becomes very important, it seems to me' (184–185). And I agree that a new stratification around class does indeed seem to become very important. After all, eventually the hero-migrant and pro-technological rhetoric work to validate a self-congratulatory fantasy for radical Italian thinkers of being the main actors in a world-spanning form of effective resistance to global capitalism. But the very possibility of perpetuating this fantasy—in essence a fantasy of transcendence—is *made possible* by global capitalism; a form of capitalism that exacerbates class differences in an exponential and particular way, namely through speeding up disenfranchisements.

I pointed out in Chapters 1 and 2 that speed-politics and the rise of the speed-elite is intrinsically related to a valorisation of connection, liberation, and border-crossing. Indeed, the desire and partial capability to cross borders, or imagining oneself to contest borders, is the result of both a discourse of transcendence (of modernism) and of an ideological erasure of the capital- and labour-intensive production processes and their exclusionary effects. Alliances with upwardly mobile migrants (often reminiscent of the 'tokenism' Foster noticed) are conceptualised as a result of the same 'authentic' desire for resistance *against* global capitalism, and a suppression of the complicities of such desires *in* capitalism. In other words, the desire for (the technologies of) speed and mobility is naturalised by projecting a false self-image of sovereignty onto a relative other, which is then wrongly imagined as a new hero for all. The result in radical Italian thought and in alter-globalist activisms dealing with migrant issues is, as we will see, that the migrant becomes the imaginary 'ideal ally' to serve the extension of neo-liberalism and its tools for the speed-elite.

This contemporary attractiveness and stickiness of the migrant metaphor shows itself in Sandra Ponzanesi's 'Diasporic Subjects and Migration.' This text is of interest here because it is one of the few pieces that critiques the migrant figuration in recent radical Italian debates in its search for an effective way to discuss migration into Europe. Ponzanesi notes that in the Italian debates, different types of migrants tend to be lumped together, despite huge differences in their backgrounds. She warns succinctly that what is problematic, 'to the extent of becoming overinflated,' is the degree to which migrants are 'celebrated as the new gurus' since they 'allow the envisioning of trespassing . . . boundaries.' She appropriately remarks that one effect of such an inflated rhetoric is that it will 'rob actual dispossessed people of their language of suffering' (207). Oddly though, in her search for analytical models that do insert axes like gender and race into studies of migration, she hails Rosi Braidotti's notion of nomadic subjectivity as helpful in envisioning female agency in migratory situations. Even though she says that Braidotti herself remains careful not to overlap her nomad with the actual migrant, Ponzanesi nonetheless does overlap the two by claiming that it is through the qualities of fluidity, fragmentation, and dislocation of the nomadic figuration that 'women enter the realm of migration as an empowering notion' (216). Her attempt to somehow insert female agency into issues of migration in Europe therefore goes full circle back into exactly what she criticised. This is because she finds the 'agency of any migrating woman' as residing in notions of fragmentation and dislocation, even though she explicitly cautions that she wishes to situate such experiences much more carefully along the relevant axes of identity. I would counter above all Ponzanesi's argument by arguing that to depict fragmentation and dislocation as empowering results not only in an erasure of the actual distinctiveness of bodily relocation but works in the service of those fortunate enough to have had such experiences as empowering ones. The exaltation of fragmentation and dislocation in Ponzanesi's text serves a similar function as the 'overinflated' migrant figuration—that of imagining the trespassing of boundaries as subversive, in this case, for 'women.' But equally, these notions say nothing about the actual disenfranchising of certain other women as an effect of fragmentation and dislocation under globalisation. The feminist standpoint in Ponzanesi's text internalises that which it claims to subsume, and erases an analysis of class from the homogenised female agency under conditions of migration. As a feminist imagination, such a position is indeed partially effective. But it is at the same time thoroughly complicit in paying tribute to the forces and technologies of globalisation that underlie fragmentation and migration. In radical Italian thought, this results in a more disingenuous erasure of its own privileges than Ponzanesi's more openly limited feminist claim. I would hence like to take on board her initial warning about the effect of migrant figurations, but extend this warning beyond purely celebratory notions of mobility, hybridity, and fragmentation.

Before I move on to critique radical Italian no-border philosophy, I must stress here again that the aim of mapping out the complicity of forging alliances in neo-liberal techno-spaces is not eventually to claim that a type of politics or activism is possible that completely does away with alliances and then become 'liberating for all.' We *cannot not* foster alliances if we want to respond to the humanist call, yet we *must also* look at the structural inequalities in our alliances, and seek a *renewed* responsibility in light of them. This is our present-day left-wing conundrum, which once more illustrates the sheer impossible stakes of all these tainted struggles: no less than the survival of certain groups and their ways of life into the next century, as these groups and their social arrangements suffer gradual erasure in a world of accelerating capitalist intensification and casualty. The activist claim to be on or to ally with 'the oppressed side' is therefore no mean feat or frivolity, and it is not my aim to denounce such a politics at all: it is a serious affair with very serious consequences indeed.

DECONSTRUCTIVE GESTURES IN RADICAL ITALIAN THOUGHT

A lot of new radical Italian thought has been printed by the independent Italian publishing house Derive Approdi, which produced a booklet called 'luoghi comuni: il movimento globale come spazio di politicizzazione' ('common places: the global movement as a space for politicisation'). This text serves as a good starting point into the framework that constitutes the imagination around the migrant. In the booklet, several authors seek to describe the state of affairs of the current anti-globalisation movement and to make claims about the direction it should and will go. They do this in a sincere attempt to tackle the imperialist logic that informed previous anti-capitalist struggles. They also try to point out and bridge the gap between theory and practice within the anti-globalisation movements. But they quickly end up depicting 'the' anti-globalisation movement as 'an open space of politicisation' whose first major cycle, where the movement supposedly moved from Seattle to Genoa, connected the resistance struggles of the 'workers in Korea, Nigeria, Brazil, and . . . in Zapatist Chiapas' (22). We see again the problematic equation of one's own activist desires with those of the Zapatistas which I discussed in Chapter 2. Here too this equation results in a false romanticisation of a highly technocratic Zapatismo as 'the' global struggle. The longed-for global unity that such alter-globalism strives for is in their view not even a utopian wish anymore, but a 'presupposed' (24) actual reality.

The use of 'presupposed' marks how 'luoghi comuni' narrates a tenuous presentism and teleological narrative of revolutionary struggle. One can recognise in such a presentism, as Fran Martin so lucidly says in 'Dismembering Theories: Working Notes,' the 'performative strategy of white, Euro-American [thought] effectively globalising marginalised categories by pronouncing them already globalised' (2). This discourse obfuscates the Eurocentric self-indulgence in *how* and *what kind of* liberation should come about—a Eurocentrism that has, as I explained in Chapter 1, segued into speed-elitism today. The anonymity also serves to universalise these notions by giving an impression of collective perspective. The authors, then, despite their admirable efforts of shedding the imperialism of previous Western activisms, relapse here in yet another kind of imperialism. The convenient myth of a yet-to-be-written space of politicisation ignores the framework in which such a space is always already cast. Whose revolution then are they talking about, and how does a diversity of other struggles get symbolically and materially appropriated in this cause? Which upwardly mobile groups and persons capable of identification with this global activist signifier are to benefit from such an empowering discourse, and who will be excluded or left behind? It is noteworthy that, for instance, Sandro Mezzadra and Fabio Raimondi, whose work I will discuss shortly, at least acknowledge in 'From Global Movement to Multitude' that the anti-globalisation movement seeks to use and enforce globalisation instead of countering it, in order to 'create a more favourable global power dissemination' (2). Although this argument has gained ground over the last few years, one is left to wonder whether such action still remains blind to the underlying mindset that is implicated by its tools, discourses, and technologies. For whom would such a 'more favourable dissemination' of power work, when it is implicated in an extremely specific pro-technological evolutionary mindset of liberation?

This unification of struggles under the umbrella of the movement in 'luoghi comuni' runs parallel with a particular revision of a Marxist anti-statism in Italian thought. This revision seems to likewise have required an adjustment of who today constitutes the 'most deserving marginal.' The problematic metaphorisation of 'migrants' and of 'the new poor' in radical Italian thought, which serves this function of most deserving other, is perhaps most blatantly present in the well-meaning work of Sandro Mezzadra.

In 'The Right to Escape,' Mezzadra tries to imagine a way of talking about migrant and refugee issues that is different from the widespread stereotyping and exclusion of (illegal) migrants, especially in the European Union, in terms of their being threats or victims. He helpfully tries to problematise the contingent nature of various geographical and national borders by invoking a language of precariousness of borders per se, and does this by redefining 'escape.' But he then turns 'escape' into some inherently political or subversive device by claiming that 'escape [is] a political category' (267). 'Escape' is simply empowering to him because it is a 'privileged way to subjectivity, a road to freedom and independence' (268). Mezzadra in turn creates a generalised notion of migrant subjectivity that is revolutionary, without recognising how migrant struggles are historically and geographically specific. Despite his correct assertion that stereotyped representations of (certain) migrants within the EU have removed 'a substantial part of the plurality of positions,' Mezzadra ventures to depict all migrants as equally oppressed and subversive, and 'the migrant condition' as having 'paradigmatic capacities' (269).

This imagination of the condition of migrants as a privileged point of view, which Mezzadra also reiterates in 'Citizenship in Motion,' perilously pretends to let someone else speak when it is actually Mezzadra's imagination that speaks. Such a flipping of the coin of victimisation in favour of the rhetoric of agency, escape, and freedom then simply repeats the same problematic. It faultily imagines victimisation as inconsistent with agency— a repetition of a typical speed-elitist dualism. To argue, as he does, that migrants 'set out on their voyages of their own will' (271) does not mean at all, as we saw with the idea of 'disguised coercion,' that they are no longer victims of certain structures of oppression. But more seriously, such an assertion erases from enquiry the violence and disenfranchisement that speed-elitism globally enacts through upholding myths that support the infrastructure of the speed-elite and the upwardly mobile. The erasure of the legacy of race in global hegemony becomes especially clear when Mezzadra talks about 'the' migrants as having the 'leading role' at the European Social Forums. He says that the forum has put 'the struggles of the last three years effectively beyond . . . the antiracist character of migration initiatives' (269), as if the Social Forums are so subversive that the issue of race has finally been overcome. Such a façade of a break with racism re-enacts racism, and corresponds to the oppressive conditions of possibility of neoliberal global meritocracy—after all, these make the equally nonsensical claim that 'anyone' can be economically successful as long as one is smart enough. Similarly, Mezzadra's discourse declares any migrant as privileged. But the privilege of their appropriation belongs primarily to him and those others who can envisage their own crossing of borders and alliances within (virtual) spaces of communication as intrinsically progressive. On the contrary, one could argue that the construction of 'new transnational social spaces' (272) through new communication and transportation technologies that Mezzadra heralds is exactly what neo-liberalism is all about.

This continuous implicit assumption of the West and the neo-liberal speed-elite as the cradle and current centre for social liberation of mankind is also present in Mezzadra and Raimondi's 'Van mondiale beweging naar multitude' ('From Global Movement to Multitude'). Calling the protests in Seattle and Genoa majestically 'the movement of movements' that strives for 'the unification of the planet' (2), Mezzadra and Raimondi talk about activists' feelings 'of pain and joy' during and after the Genoa protests as 'comparable in intensity to the feelings after 9/11' (1). They go on to claim that all kinds of past libratory struggles, from feminist to environmentalist, are now all unified under the sign of 'the big struggle.' This mistakenly makes, for instance, anti-sexist activism congruous with global anti-capitalist activism. They problematically render the image of the new communication technologies as the one neutral tool that 'all these groups so skilfully use.' The 'body of migrants' gets represented as a body that *signifies* the required subversion of boundaries within the capitalist global system:

> The migration movement, with the elements of subjectivity they take with them, were this year really one big laboratory of the 'globalisation from below'. Under our eyes they developed a genealogy . . . They create a dramatic tension between the cosmopolitan demands for freedom of movement and the insurrection of new borders . . . If the movement really wants to provide an alternative, then it should recognise in the migrant the meaning of its incentives as well as the most important form of subjectivity. (2, 4)

The problem here is again that migrants are portrayed as inhabiting some sort of radically different subjectivity, as if subjectivity is an unchangeable internal object they carry around. Many radical Italian texts and their derivatives likewise speak of 'new subjectivities.' Newness indeed often functions under neo-liberalism as a marker of coolness, progress, and success. In the interview 'Neither Here nor Elsewhere,' Brett Neilson asks Mezzadra why migration has become such a prominent issue of concern within the World Social Forums and subsequently within Italian thought. Mezzadra explains that at the G8 protests in Genoa, there was a 'large rally organised by migrants that was a big success' (1). This success made them organise a topic at the European Social Forum (ESF) that criticised the European Schengen Agreements on new border policies within the EU, in order to oppose national and European border policies 'as a matter of principle.' Describing how the previous victimisation of migrants within the anti-globalisation movement has been paternalistic and 'merely' resulted in assistance, care, and protection, Mezzadra suggests that the new image of the migrant is instead one which represents 'migrants as the central protagonists of current processes of global transformation' (4).

Once more, Mezzadra flips the coin of victimisation in favour of a heroic and homogeneous figuration of the migrant and its 'new subjectivity.' What is significant in this flipping process is how dismissively Mezzadra speaks of the idea of (needing) care in favour of a rather limited individualist (and arguably masculinist) notion of personhood as always capable and enabled. This narrative perpetuates the typical imperialist strategy of 'speaking for' a certain group at the ESF, instead of letting them speak, whoever that unproblematic 'them' is. It does so through coining 'them' as 'protagonists,' and through the theoretical fallacy that being 'an agent' is a direct challenge to neo-liberalism. Such a deception validates the humanist fantasy of objective knowledge and control. Mezzadra employs the same trick of pretending to let 'them' speak in 'Citizenship in Motion.' He repeats the claim here that 'the condition of migrants constitutes a privileged point from which to observe . . . the trend to decompose citizenship' (2). The migrant becomes a symbol for the 'cool' subjectivity desired by Mezzadra. This completely glosses over the specific situated desires and struggles of individual migrants, as well as over the economic and political contexts that caused them to flee or migrate. To equate migrant subjectivities with subversive force is a rhetorical ploy, serving a one-dimensional demonisation of borders as thwarting the transcendental desires of the subject. And the speed-elite thrives on the fantasy to eliminate such borders and to 'unify the planet,' a fantasy which Mezzadra pursues. Mezzadra's discourse recognises only those few migrants who are upwardly mobile enough to join the speed-elite. We could perhaps argue that border-hacker Fran Illich is upwardly mobile in this sense.

The pervasive heroisation of the migrant in Italian thought can be traced back more in detail to the influential 1996 article 'Beyond Human Rights' by Giorgio Agamben. In this article, Agamben moves away from the classical notion of 'workers and human rights' upon which a lot of Marxist and left-wing thought and praxis was—and continues to be—based. Such a critique of 'rights' is very valuable in a climate in which various activisms, as for instance Lovink and Schneider's case for the 'basic human right to communicate,' work in utter consonance with capitalist disenfranchisement. However, Agamben also claims that '[we should] build our political philosophy anew starting from the one and only figure of the refugee' (159) because the latter fruitfully 'represents a disquieting element in the order of the Nation-State' (161). Here too his description imagines the refugee as a metaphorical breaker of (in this case national) judicial boundaries, without realising that for certain refugees the affirmation of territorial or bodily boundaries may be exactly what they need or want. It is particularly telling that a lot high-tech no-border campaigns and migrant heroisations, like 'No Borders, No Nations' in *we are everywhere*, go hand in hand with anti-nation or anti-state rhetoric. The technology of nation, and thus the existence of migration (as moving into another nation), is after all closely related to the initial spread of colonialism and the subsequent solidification of neo-colonialism *as* neo-liberal capitalism through technological control.

Agamben appropriates 'the refugee' for his own Marxist fight against the capitalist state. But while it is one thing to point out the material and judicial poverty of *certain* migrants, it is quite another issue to build a whole politics on the hero figure of the migrant or refugee whose particularity is lost in favour of unification strategies against the state or capitalism. Worse still, such a strategy unwittingly plays into the hands of those who wish to be the unbounded and mobile saviours of marginality. Indeed, the radicals of the industrial nations want to *be* the Third World here. Without a doubt, such a revealing discourse by Mezzadra and Agamben posits the extremely mobile and flexible individual, enabled by globalisation and communication technologies, as an ideal figure. In the meantime, it also imagines itself as a truly subversive and liberating politics, at the centre of the socio-economic realm. Not incidentally, their fantasy of the ideal subject rings very close to the actual real-life experiences of many well-meaning academics and activists, who communicate incessantly online and travel regularly to other ends of the world to protest or discuss global problems.

The idea of the migrant as always in opposition to capitalism or the state (which state exactly, one should ask) falsely creates 'capital' or 'the state' as an a-historical and undifferentiated locus of oppression.[14] This idea is constantly present in Hardt and Negri's work, as well as in several other radical Italian texts which I will leave aside here.[15] In Hardt and Negri's work it results in an emphasis on 'exodus' as the only possible solution against global dominance. We saw already that a demonisation of the state also drives Mezzadra's 'opposing European borders as a matter of principle,' and segues into more all-encompassing fantasies of deleting borders and limits. The simplistic depiction of resistance as outside the state paves the way for a neo-humanist rhetoric which in effect perpetuates the historically and geographically *specific* modes of oppression under nationalist and capitalist conditions of possibility.[16] Not surprisingly, then, Agamben ends his diatribe against the nation-state and for the exemplification of the refugee by arguing for the existence of a few political communities within the same state but 'in exodus from each other.' He claims that this would lead to the 'European cities rediscover[ing] their ancient vocation [*sic*] as cities of the world' (164). Such grand nostalgia for Europe's old glorious cities glosses over the colonialist and patriarchal horrors that have been inflicted in the name of those so-called cities of the world. This combination of Marxism and relativism is also very similar to many 'radical democracy' writings— the French counterpart of radical Italian thought—like those of Ernesto Laclau and Chantal Mouffe. Both schools install a humanist discourse of self-determination not for the individual but for some completely undifferentiated kind of 'community.' This community is in turn represented as having itself certain Enlightenment capabilities, as if that community itself were a coherent autonomous agent. One could perhaps read such an increase of theorising 'communities in exodus from each other' in recent European left-wing radical thought as crisis-managing the failure of the rhetoric of multi-culturalism so pervasive in the 1980s. It nonetheless inadvertently repeats the same problematic of the discourse of multi-culturalism: a forged unity through pretending to allow for real differences.

OF MIGRANTS AND POOR FOLKS

Let me next turn to an extraordinary example of the pervasive romanticisation of the migrant in academic and activist thought: Hardt and Negri's *Empire*. *Empire* is such an exceptional case because it managed to successfully claim the status of the 'bible' of the alter-globalisation movement, and I myself vividly recall being enraptured by its prose. The success of this book suggests immediately the resonance it must have with the new imperatives of acceleration that many activists find themselves caught up in. Modernist and classist presuppositions of 'the' global libertarian struggles and a post-modern attempt at describing an emergent heterogeneous mass come together in *Empire* in the notion of 'the multitude.' The term serves a similar strategy within radical Italian thought at large. If 'the migrant' is the individualist rendition of the fantasy of transcendence, then the multitude is its supposed communal hero. The term was actually coined by Baruch Spinoza to describe the fact that to conceive of the individual as an autonomous agent fails to take into account the necessarily uneven material and symbolical distribution and interdependent relations of 'the self.' Negri in 'M as in Multitude' instead conceives of it as an 'irreducible multiplicity' (111). Whereas this conception without doubt seeks to describe the absolute differences between individuals in a given social field, it constantly slips into a form of relativism in service of some globally perceived anti-capitalism. This is because Hardt and Negri do not at all attest to or profess to the differential axes of oppression, like sexism and racism, which traverse this multitude.[17] The term becomes a fortification of a vision of the subject as in control, through implicitly attesting to liberation in a totally singular way. In 'Revolutions That as Yet Have No Model,' Spivak in fact recognises that such a manoeuvre, common to alter-globalist thought, constitutes an 'individualism more or less disguised as pluralism' (101). It is not surprising that the conveniently abstract term 'multitude' has been happily appropriated by cyber-utopianists like Geert Lovink in the form of 'digital multitudes' as I pointed out in Chapter 2.

Hardt and Negri claim in *Empire* that the new world order results in the creation of a 'global proletariat.' This creation, they argue, unifies all subjects under late capitalism as there is no place external to its logic—an assessment with which I almost agree. But they conflate the idea of the 'virtual' space with notions of 'being, loving, transforming and creating that reside in the multitude' (357). They suggest that the diffuse space of cyberspace has facilitated the coming to strength of the emancipatory desires that 'naturally' reside in the multitudes. This fantasy again completely overlooks the materially violent and exclusivist histories and effects of new technologies. And more importantly, Hardt and Negri ignore the question of how an internally *differing* multitude could possibly have constituents who share the exact *same* desire for change. The reason for this essentialist assertion is that Hardt and Negri conceive of original Renaissance humanism as a system that, when properly installed, will lead to a state in which 'No transcendental power or measure will determine the values of our world. Value will be determined only by humanity's own continuous innovation and creation' (356).

Not only is this statement stunningly nostalgic and naïve; it more seriously generates a highly exclusionist and Eurocentric image of personhood as an Enlightenment subject proper. That subject would be capable of—or even primarily born for—self-constitution, active creation, and expression of his individual 'free will.' This kind of patriarchal essentialism serves to justify the neo-liberal rhetoric that has emerged from Eucken's ideas, which hinges on transcendentalist aspirations that everything and everybody should and will ultimately be free-flowing. But anybody's 'free flow' can today only be the *result* of neo-liberalism. It is therefore hardly surprising that Hardt and Negri find in the mobility of migrants their image of the ideal global subversive protagonist, when they claim in *Empire* that 'The postcolonial hero is the one who continually transgresses territorial and racial boundaries, who destroys particularisms and points towards a common civilization' (363). This heroisation once more renders invisible actual migrants and the violence of certain local and global inequities that made them migrate. It also serves once more as the rhetorical foundation for a false unification of what constitutes current lives and struggles. This is not to say that some individuals who identify as migrant or refugee do not occasionally make use of these rhetorical 'handgrips' provided by such intellectual thought. As we can see, within certain sections of the European and World Social Forums some upwardly mobile migrants have cunningly done so. But such cunning points exactly to the fact that this subject-metaphor in Italian thought is complicit with the institutions and technologies of subjugation that are available under speed.

Hardt and Negri also replicate the mis-interpretations made by certain North American techno-utopian academics of Deleuze and Guattari's desiring machines. The conflation of the virtual with the desires of the multitudes equates the actual Internet and its polarising global economic system as a 'smooth space' for alliance and transformation, as if it were the materialisation of Deleuze and Guattari's rhizome. This conflation assumes that the constituents of the multitude somehow long for one and the same thing: the desire to free oneself from any constraint. Hardt and Negri erroneously talk about the Internet as an 'unlimited number of interconnected nodes with no central point of control . . . This is what Deleuze and Guattari called a rhizome' (299). In a similar vein, they transform Donna Haraway's ambivalent cyborg[18] into a utopian emblem (218). Michael Rustin hints lucidly at the reasons for the widespread success of *Empire* within the European and American alter-globalisation movement and no-borders activists in 'Empire: A Postmodern Theory of Revolution.' Rustin suggests that 'the political appeal of their analysis, its natural constituency so to speak, is to those called by "desire" in its various forms, and moved by hostility to restriction and restraint . . . Global capitalism has been the bringer of this condition of freedom' (9). Indeed, the irony is that, while Hardt and Negri *explicitly* seek to exhibit a post-modern Marxism in their book, they *implicitly* herald global capitalism and its hyper-modern technologies as the one condition which allows the (digital) multitudes to make allies and liberate themselves. Hardt and Negri have no eye for either their own complicity within capitalism's neo-colonisation through the material and discursive acceleration of Eurocentrism, nor for the massive resource- and people-intensive labour that this speed-elitist infrastructure requires.[19]

The romanticisation and the false identification with the supposedly subversive qualities of 'the' migrants attain almost grotesque forms in Hardt and Negri's sequel to *Empire*, called *Multitude: War and Democracy in the Age of Empire*. Not only do they again overlap the idea of 'networked resistances' with the 'subversive power of the multitude;' they also go to great lengths to locate such subversive powers of the multitude primarily in 'the poor' (85–89). This is because the poor supposedly 'embody the ontological condition not only of resistance but also of productive life itself' (133). This is obviously a questionable exotic depiction. Later on they even posit 'the migrants' as a subset of the poor. The migrant constitutes, according to them, 'a special category of the poor that demonstrates this wealth and productivity' of resistance and life. Present-day migration gets opposed to the great European migrations of the past that were directed into 'empty spaces.' They argue that current migrations move into 'fullness' because the 'economies need them' and because migrants themselves are 'full.' Hardt and Negri negate the presence of other peoples and the violent colonialist overtaking in the areas previous Europeans migrated to. More seriously, they actually support a condition which foremost benefits the speed-elite by not questioning these 'full' economies. And Hardt and Negri's blatant appropriation of the migrant in favour of exalting anything or anyone that is networked and mobile, while simultaneously completely mistaking production for subversion, does not stop here. They also project onto the migrants a vague desire for 'something more, their refusal to accept the way things are' (133), without acknowledging how a 'desire for something more' may lie at the base of consumerism. Identifying such a desire in 'migrants' says absolutely nothing about such a desire's believed quality of contesting neo-liberalism—it simply dissimulates the *constitutive* relationship between those desires and the reinforcement of neo-liberal globalisation.

In the same way, Negri negates the potentially illuminating analysis of this constitutive relationship in his debate 'Empire and Multitude: A Dialogue on the New Order of Globalisation' with Danilo Zolo. Zolo is correctly suspicious of many of *Empire*'s rhetoric around the poor and the multitude. He even says that the 'emphatic exaltations of the power of the multitude . . . [appears] indebted to Marxist messianism and its grandiose political simplifications' (11). Zolo also points out that *Empire* seems 'animated by a real technological fervour.' But Zolo does not manage to put his finger on what such a discourse on migrants as well as the new information technologies effectuates, and how it is complicit in perpetuating neo-liberal technocratic conditions. Negri therefore unabashedly continues his dangerous exoticisations by claiming that 'the migrant has the dignity of those who search for truth, production and happiness' (12) and that the 'information revolution provides . . . new spaces for freedom' (11). This nostalgia for the migrant is again founded on the well-intended claim, which also we saw with Mezzadra, that we must oppose the previous victimisation of the migrants and instead see them as 'actors.' But as with Mezzadra's misconception of escape, the opposition of victims and agents is dualistic, and leaves no space for the urgent analysis of how agency, empowerment, and subjectivity are in fact embedded in pervasive speed-elitist structures and legacies.

Those who eventually benefit from such hyper-modernist rhetoric are those who can romantically identify with the desire to be free and mobile. These people can imagine that they are themselves subversive or liberating elements within globalisation, without suffering the dire consequences of technocratic globalisation. Once more, speed-elitism perpetuates itself in the avowal that the radicals of the industrial nations want to be the Third World. This desire to be the oppressed also emanates from the section in *Multitude* which is offensively titled 'The Wealth of the Poor (or, We Are the Poors!)' (129). The exaltation of migration throughout *Empire* and *Multitude* serves to support and enhance the tools and discourses for the speed-elite. It simultaneously appeals to the vanity of the Western alter-globalist reader who imagines him- or herself at the centre of liberatory change by playing out his or her desire, constituted by humanist neo-liberalism, for identifying in migrants the 'real' margins. As we will see shortly, the speed-elitist projection of desire, backed up with radical Italian thought, plays a distinct role in many contemporary activist interventions in refugee issues.

Finally, any feminist reader of *Empire* and *Multitude* may feel that the 'multitude' and 'the migrant' force feminist and anti-racist struggles under the umbrella of anti-capitalism, while effectively silencing them. The only reference to feminism is successfully buried in a footnote in *Empire* that says: 'In fact . . . we would say that the most profound and solid problematic that has yet been elaborated for the critique of bio-politics is found in feminist theory' (422, note 17). Though briefly mentioning the feminist critique of the European 'workerist' schools as 'perhaps' a good way to re-evaluate their and other anti-capitalist analyses, Hardt and Negri do not go into this at all in *Empire*. They keep projecting a particular contemporary European and technocratic obsession on some vague sort of global, uniform, and supposedly subversive mass.

NO-BORDER THEORIES, ITALIAN THOUGHT, AND NEW-MEDIA ACTIVISM

The utopian fantasy of the subject transgressing boundaries that I detected in Agamben, Mezzadra and Raimondi, and Hardt and Negri fits eerily well with the imaginations of new media activists and their rather Christian self-construction as 'saviours of marginality.' This in turn corresponds well with the promises and faculties of the new communication and transportation technologies that the global speed-elitist hegemony needs and endorses. The depictions of new technologies in radical Italian thought are totally in step with much of the American cyber-happy and neo-liberal discourses on technologies. This makes one wonder how 'radical' these ideas really are, and begs the question why so many activists like me believe in such radicality.

As I suggested in Chapter 2, Lovink and Schneider's new media activist 'Reverse Engineering Freedom' and 'A Virtual World Is Possible' make several references of new technologies as somehow emancipatory in the face of migratory issues. The rhetoric in 'Reverse Engineering Freedom' bases itself largely on some supposedly authentic 'irresistible drive towards freedom.' This rhetoric facilitates overlapping the 'freedom of communication' and 'freedom of movement'—of course, all inspired by the Internet, the technology of progress *par excellence*. They even call free communication a 'precious human right' (5), proclaim border management and digital management a 'farce' (4), and liken Internet tracking and hyper-linking to the actual trafficking of humans, all of which are according to them subversive practices (6). This dissimulation of the material consequences of borders, and of the miseries of trafficking and the privileges of high-tech tracking, serves their own aspiration of being 'no longer slaves of territory' (5). This dissimulation is exactly also present in radical Italian thought. Moreover, (digital) border management is hardly a 'farce' but facilitates Lovink and Schneider's privileged movements and rhetoric of passing borders, as well as the detection and detention technologies that incarcerate and occasionally kill refugees and asylum seekers. To claim that 'free communication' is a human right, as Spivak notes in 'Pax Electronica,' is rather 'spelling out the importance of finance capital' (77). This is because it imposes those new media technologies that flash capital requires as a must-have for everyone in order for capital to colonise all territories. It is this colonisation and intensification which in turn *cause* migratory flows of all sorts, which Lovink and Schneider uncritically sell as 'freedom.' Likewise, in 'A Virtual

World Is Possible,' Lovink and Schneider simply equate 'open sources, open borders, open knowledge' as the same (3). They even claim that 'The new ethical-aesthetic paradigm lives on in . . . the nerdish attitude of a digital working class [and] in the omnipresence of migrant struggles and other border-crossing experiences' (3). Such 'brilliance of everyday experience get[s] dramatically lost in the academification of radical left theory' (4), as if such 'nerdish' digitally enhanced border-crossing is an ethical contestation of neo-liberalism. I on the contrary suggest firstly that (digital) border-crossing is the result of speed-structures, and secondly that opposing such 'everyday' digital experience with academic practices is a dichotomy exemplary of speed-politics. The idea that activism is somehow not confined by the limits of theorisation overlaps conspicuously well with the deceptive idea of the Internet as unconditional space. This dichotomy also agrees with the acceleration of politics as mere transactions I discussed in Chapter 2. The obsession with the migrant and with border-crossing is then not characteristic of radical Italian thought alone, but is also common in new media activism. This shows the intrinsic links between all these viral practices under acceleration.

Not surprisingly, other radical Italians have exploited the new-media-activist argument. In 'Radical Machines against the Techno-Empire,' Matteo Pasquinelli exhibits techno-optimism when claiming that the anti-globalisation movement should expand on and radicalise the ideas of the free software movement and its slogan 'information wants to be free.' In a move comparable to the new-media-activist circle's popular notion from Bey of the 'temporary autonomous zone' as the 'subversive web in the dominant net,' Pasquinelli says that the Internet is part of a larger network of human communications that simply can be divided in 'good' and 'bad' collective intelligences (1). On the side of the 'good collectives' are all the global movements, under which according to him fall also the free-software movement, the academic knowledge-sharing community, the Creative Commons project for art and knowledge sharing (which has websites in the United States and Italy), and the precarious workers movements. Pasquinelli avoids the term 'multitudes' for this grouping, because he considers the concept 'more useful to exorcise the identitary pretences of the global movement, than as a constructive tool' (2). Whereas I seriously doubt whether the term has exorcised these pretences in any way, Pasquinelli just as much ends up simplifying 'the' global situation into a movie-like match between 'radical machines versus imperial techno-monsters.' He does this through projecting both the 'good' and the 'bad' collective intelligences onto networked communication spaces. This splitting of technological discourses of the present and the future into utopias and dystopias inhabited by two oppositional homogeneous groups fails to acknowledge how such discourses (and their subjects) are in fact intertwined. Pasquinelli writes himself and his fellow media activists into the margins, while remaining blind to the amount of privilege, access, and (cultural) capital individuals that meddle with new technologies have. His text serves a sort of exorcising activity. This is because the possible unease over the *complicity* of the free-software movement and of other media activism in the violent expansion of neo-liberalism gets suppressed by projecting its own ideological violence on the fantasy of 'bad collective intelligences.'

The entanglements of these romanticisations of migrants and its complicit cyber-happy push for the virtualisation of communications and economics are also present in the fact that much of the European and Australian no-border activist writings, similar to Mezzadra's work, get published on the technophile *MakeWorlds* website. The theme of this website is the geeky phrase 'border=0, location=yes.'[20] The Australian new media organisation and website *fibreculture*, which is committed to the building of a public info-structure through Internet technologies, has hosted various events around ideas of the multitude.[21] *MakeWorlds* hosts a number of articles that equate the faculties of new technologies, in their border-crossing and accelerating functions, with the alleviation of migratory miseries. Many of these theories and Australian activities rely on the work of radical Italian thinkers, much like their European counterparts. A good example is the work of Angela Mitropoulos, an engaged activist-intellectual who has been at the cradle of the Australian no-border initiative xborder. While I share Mitropoulos's concern for refugees, she performs in the *MakeWorlds* essay 'Movements against Enclosures: Virtual Is Preamble' a misappropriation of Deleuze's nomadism (which she dubs 'techno-nomadism') similar to the misreading of the 'rhizome' invoked by Hardt and Negri. She suggests that the Internet is antagonistic to 'authorised' spatial organisation, and that therefore virtual space is a precursor of a more general breaking down of or 'escape' from hierarchies and borders. Migrant movements, says Mitropoulos, therefore first became visible in cyberspace, because migrants as well as cyberspace invoke Deleuzian 'lines of flight and escape' (1, 2). Her misreading of the Deleuzian concept of nomadism and celebration of 'the' migratory experience is also reminiscent of Bey's idea of 'psychic nomadism' in his *The Temporary Autonomous Zone*. Bey lumps all kinds of 'moving' people together under this header of psychic nomadism—tourists, migrants, people who 'travel via the Net,' refugees, and even homeless people, who all inhabit 'a multi-perspectived post-ideological worldview able to move "rootlessly" from philosophy to tribal myth, from natural science to Taoism' (409). Bey performs exactly the lumping together that Ponzanesi warned against, which is, of course, as I discussed in Chapter 2, far from post-ideological. On the contrary, it effortlessly erases any analysis of production and class differences required for privileging those he short-sightedly calls 'all of us, living through our automobiles and our TVs' (410). I agree completely with John Armitage in 'Ontological Anarchy, The Temporary Autonomous Zone, and the Politics of Cyber-culture' that Bey's ideology in effect comprises some 'extravagant form of liberal individualism' (4). Bey self-indulgently imagines his desires for transcendence and pleasure as subversive, and its connections with refugees as liberatory.

Despite her welcome criticism of exclusionary institutions, Mitropoulos continues with an analogous set of problematic techno-metaphors. In 'The Micro-Physics of Theoretical Production and Border-Crossings,' she tackles Jason Read's *The Micro-Politics of Capital,* which argues that resistance under late capitalism is interior to power. This posits the question for Mitropoulos of what then is the use of resistant practices like migrant activism, or even of critical reading and writing, when such practices are inevitably part of the capitalist production of migration. Mitropoulos desperately recuperates no-border activisms as subversive in light of the 'irreducibility' of resistance to capitalism. She implausibly claims, referencing Negri's idea of the multitude as subversive, that 'crossing the border' remains a 'critical practice' (2) because it is a physical movement instead of a result of the capitalist subjugation as 'immaterial worker' (6). But I counter that the argument of physical movement does not at all ward off the spectre of capitalism *producing* such movement. Mitropoulos also likens border-crossing experiences and critical writings of the no-border groups with the displacing qualities of the Net regarding critical intellectual practice (5). She misses the opportunity to critically reflect on the 'conjunction between newer forms of work and communication and undocumented movement by adopting the language and topography of the net' (1) that she correctly notices.

The problems of Mitropoulos's work are very similar to those we saw with Mezzadra, and Hardt and Negri. What she fails to understand is that empowerment exists *in* the complicities she (and other upwardly mobile migrants) engage in, in this case through the available speed-elitist imagination of depicting new technologies and their transcendence of national borders as subversive. Calling the movements of undocumented migrants 'autonomous' is therefore a misconstruction; such movements are extremely dependent on available capital, infrastructure, or even good health to travel, as well as on the pull of the existence of certain borders inside of which a 'free' and safe space to work and live is guaranteed for privileged migrants. Her claim that the 'beliefs' that circulate under postmodern production are completely 'irrelevant' (3) is therefore erroneous. Her analysis in fact shows that it is precisely the rhetoric of mobility, technological progress, and transcendence that is increasingly the only *myth* available for resistant imagination. She applauds the alliances between immaterial workers and illegal immigrants in the xborder practices, while failing to notice how such an uneven alliance is a hierarchical product of late capitalism. This is not to say that all these initiatives around erasing borders may not be well intended and insightful, but that these intentions are much more complicit in the spread of neo-liberal globalisation than they wish to be. These initiatives will therefore sadly have effects that are accelerating global class, gender, and racial hierarchies, and will not bring about what they justly hope for.

READY TO DELETE THE BORDER?

The expansion of the spaces and tools of the speed-elite through the rendition of refugees and migrants as 'most oppressed' and as subversive symbols of border-crossing returns in the concrete practices of many alter-globalist groups that deal with migrant issues. Many of these activisms are suspiciously in tune with the cyber-happy rhetoric of un-hierarchical networking, free flows, and trans-nationalism, like, for instance, the name Anti-Racist Group for Free Flooding already suggests. These groups physically use the Internet as a main tool for communication and alliance building, using the problematic discourse of 'open spaces.' The well-intended No-Borders network website is, for instance, full of talk of mobility, breaking down borders, and freedom from constraints. It does not or cannot recognise that it is the very constraints that make media activism or citizenship, which migrants or refugees may desire, possible in the first place. The simplistic myth of freedom versus constraint returns with devastating effects in certain no-border activities. For instance, in Europe in early 2004, refugees were helped to escape from a detention centre, after which the refugees had no other option than to turn themselves in again because their 'liberators' had not thought at all of what to do next, after that wonderful 'setting them free.'[22] The 'freedom' of being outside of legislation and unrecognised by borders is, as many refugees may be able to tell you, not really a position to be desired.

Another instance of how no-border activism turns out to be detrimental for some of the actual migrants involved is the 'civil disobedience' actions around the former Australian detention centre Woomera. In the Easter of 2002, a large caravan of activists, complete with their ad hoc Indymedia centre dubbed desert.indymedia,[23] gathered for a number of protest rallies at Woomera. During one of the protests several detainees managed to get out of the confinement by climbing over the barbed-wire fences while the activists were chanting 'freedom, freedom.' The outbreak is described in very emotional terms by the caravan participants. Activists said that the detainees were 'crying for freedom' and that a number of detainees 'reached out to touch our hands.' Such stories obviate the enormous yearning of the activists in the idea of 'freeing' the detainees. One of the participants, Kanthi Lewis, tellingly wrote that they were 'making the journey [to Woomera] to discover our humanity in the liberation of those who have been dehumanised.' Whereas the activist heart is here again indisputably in the right place, it nonetheless also shows how the caravan worked as a form of redemption and reinstallation of the humanist idea of 'liberation' for the participants. Another participant, Jess White, in the same way says in 'We Are Human Beings: The Woomera Breakout' that 'their first instinct was to convince us they were human . . . we discovered, amidst the horror, a common humanity' (430). An Afghan refugee, Chang, serves in White's story as the 'other' who functions as the responsive mirror for the activist ego I spoke of when discussing the problems of solidarity. Chang is said to be 'fighting for his freedom' and 'asked us for one thing: solidarity' (435). Even when Chang gets dragged back into Woomera because White and her fellow activists had no plan after the emotional destruction of the initial Woomera fence (about which she later learned they could have walked around!), White says that Chang's last words were: 'Even if we are arrested, we are happy we saw outside the fence' (436). Her translation of Chang's predicament into a personal activist victory in favour of romantic ideas of 'freedom' circumvents that Chang was there to acquire Australian citizenship (not 'freedom,' but a status of asylum within the empowering and oppressive borders of one nation). It is interesting that White admits that the tearing down of the first fence—the one they could have walked around—served a strong symbolic function. Its symbolism informed all the rest of the activists' high-adrenaline actions, as well as her writing a narrative of 'escape' as ultimate liberatory goal in 'We Are Human Beings.'

In 'Restore the Commons! Break the Borders!' White continues to discuss migrant activism in terms of the (again decontextualised) Zapatista standpoint of 'the war of capitalism against humanity.'[24] Though accurately sketching how migrants today cannot be 'political trophies' like in the era of the Cold War, when people fled to the West from communist states and were hailed as examples that showed capitalism was a better system, she nonetheless argues vaguely that migrants are 'part of the resistance of the side Marcos termed humanity.' She also mistakenly says that migrants refuse 'to be redefined as labour power' (3). She even claims that this type of resistance is 'within every one of us' (3). One wonders whether White realises what makes many migrants migrate, which is often precisely a 'desire to be redefined as labour power' though with a better salary and more useful citizenship. Her narrative therefore affirms Spivak's comment in *A Critique of Postcolonial Reason* that capitalism generates 'the subaltern as the rhetoric of their protests' (373). It assumes that the subaltern shares the same aspirations of resistance and 'humanity' as the activist, which means paradoxically that the migrant, despite her or his heroisation as radical other, in the end shares the same desire *for* the capitalism that made them migrate. White's conclusion appears as an extension of the Cold War propaganda she earlier refuted, because it plays out the rhetoric of freedom and resistance through 'migrant propaganda' in a parallel way. The card of neo-liberalism as virtuous is therefore often easily and smartly played by corporate elites in the name of humanity. The clear-cut opposition between an evil neo-liberalism and some enlightened notion of 'humanity' that White sketches therefore does not hold. Spivak actually noticed this in 'The Rest of the World': 'The other side is going to win the argument very easily if you say it is commodification. They say, "What do you mean? We are acknowledging that these are communicating subjects" ' (179). Again, this collapse of human existence and communication flows shows that the project of humanism is in dire straits due to its morphing into speed.

It is typical that almost none of the stories on Woomera2002 are told by the (ex)detainees themselves. There exists in its place a plethora of activist impressions online. Most of the activist eyewitness stories end with emotional accounts of that day but do not go into what happened with the detainees in the weeks after. In addition, a striking aspect of these stories is that they are always narrating in terms of a 'we' (the helpers) opposed to a 'they' (the victims).[25] As in the European case, none of the activists at Woomera had really thought of what to do after those refugees escaped from the camp. In the months that followed, the Australian government decided to close Woomera and transport all the detainees to the tightly guarded high-tech Baxter detention centre, as well as to several camps on islands north of the Australian mainland. So much for improving the lot of the detainees. Mitropoulos mentions on Indymedia Sydney that the civil disobedience action was 'audacious, but . . . impractical,' but still does not go into details nor into a reflection of what urged the activists to read the misery of the crying detainees as a 'cry for freedom' that could simply be obtained by 'helping them out' in this way. This does not mean that refugee detention centres are not highly problematic institutions in which people often live in horrible conditions, but that a simple destruction of fences, or the elimination or traversing of borders in general, as always liberating is misguided. On the contrary, many of the (new) refugees were perhaps worse off after the action, *thanks to* those technologies of mobility and communication.

There exists no proper analysis in no-border activism of how 'we' can live in luxury, cross certain borders, and enjoy new technologies *because* 'they' can (partly) not. The widening gap between rich and poor, the ongoing feminisation of poverty, and the disenfranchisement of people worldwide, which makes some of them migrate in search for a better life (if they have the means to do so), is a *result* of exactly those humanist desires for more 'freedom' that lie at the base of late-capitalist globalisation and technological innovation. No-border activisms are blind to how these discourses of migration and mobility work in tandem with the increasing neoliberalisation in favour of the speed-elite, and simply keep promoting new technologies as tools that transgress borders. Indeed, Mitropoulos mentions in 'Flotilla of Hope Update' on Indymedia Sydney that the Internet is of main importance to the No-Border and xborder actions. She does not comprehend the relationship between the conditions of possibility that surround the Internet and the increasing implementation of high-tech surveillance gear around camps like Baxter. In 'The Micro-Physic of Theoretical Production and Border-Crossings,' Mitropoulos draws once more on the work of Hardt and Negri, to wrongly conclude that 'crossing the border is a permanent condition of critical practice' (6). But such is quite clearly exactly what the current academic, activist, and business elites, who travel to meetings, protests, and conferences worldwide, and who merrily participate in the 'spectacle of resistance' and progress, would love to hear. No-border examples hence show that the activists' desire to overcome neoliberalism is *structurally situated within the very spaces of acceleration.* These activisms therefore in effect reproduce the speed-hierarchies they hope to contest. This means that any story of successfully and intentionally effectuating change is in the end a masked repetition of the same.

FROM MOBILITY TO GLOBALITY

The current obsession with the migrant or the refugee in radical Italian thought, as well as in the alter-globalisation movement and in academic and policymaking institutions, points at a peculiar new mode of production of 'the most deserving marginal' under speed-elitism. Many policy institutions problematically depict the migrant (and, of course, only the migrant from certain regions, or with certain skin colour or religious beliefs) as a problem or object. But the migrant is also problematically rendered into a unified symbol of subversion in much Italian radical writing, much like the notion of the mestiza or nomad is de-contextualised and appropriated in a lot of activist and academic thought. The migrant metaphor primarily makes possible the claim for some sort of hegemonic struggle in 'the new world order' by radical Italian thinkers. They do so through a doubly romanticising move, leading to the reproduction of the migrant or refugee as a heroic figure, as well as the acting out of a *desire* for self-identification of these writers with the migrant. This works through claims that s/he embodies the transcendental fantasy of the total subsumption of boundaries. We can conclude that the romanticised rendition of the migrant or refugee as quintessential boundary breaker is a dangerous distortion. This distortion works in service of self-valorising fantasies around the ideal native informant. These fantasies stem from those who already are the winners in the global sphere, and can afford to take up a position as saviours of marginality. Because ultimately, it is not at all national or judicial borders that migrants or refugees inherently contest.

Migrants as a rule aspire to be empowered *by certain* borders by actively wanting to be subjugated within them. In other words, most migrants seek that much-needed citizen status as well as care, safety, and a chance to earn a decent income, in order to gain possible access to speed-elite status (or in order to make the American Dream come true, like Illich). Rather than being some authentic force that precedes or subverts national or bodily borders, the refugee or migrant is victim *and* agent within a complex and heterogeneous logic of speed—within the diverse forms of violence done by national borders, as these seek to re-inscribe their internal and peripheral laws and regulations. Any politics that builds on the depiction of the migrant as some sort of subversive hero reproduces the speed-elitist fantasy of existence without borders by substituting objectification for romanticisation. Such politics obscures the violent sexist and racist history and present situation of the material and technological conditions of this depiction. This 'hallucination of radical alterity' that is the migrant therefore functions in service of the global speed-elite.[26] The exponential use of technologies of mobility, connection, and border-crossing by this elite has disseminated the myth of 'freedom.' And it was and is exactly from the often violent militaristic, technological, and material re-inscription and expansion of such hyper-modern myths that many refugees suffer. Romanticising the migrant as ideal other is thus an identity politics which re-enacts former militarisms and imperialisms, even if the romanticisation of the migrant or refugee is informed by a benevolent wish to oppose victimisation and the erasure of actual migratory experiences. But the turning upside down of this opposition wrongly suggests that migrants cannot be elites or that agency cannot imply victimisation. It also erroneously assumes that creating a 'mirror subject' of neo-liberalism will bring the latter down. Exactly the opposite is the case: the romanticisation of the migrant is thoroughly complicit in neo-liberal capital, because it celebrates mobility, speed, new technologies, and transcendence, and hence solidifies the hegemony of *certain* nation-states.

What is therefore really at play in these narratives is a 'jealousy' in the name of humanism, an affirmation of speed-structures one resists so as to keep the idea alive that one *can* somehow overcome those structures. But if this is true of the new media and migrant activisms and theories I have discussed in the last three chapters, then this must also be true of the production of my own narrative that 'seeks to describe the truth' about those activisms and the fundamental appeal to acknowledge widespread humanitarian and ecological disaster from a largely theoretical position. What is more, we can safely conclude from the last two chapters that the setting to work of post-structuralism and activism once more hinges on speed-discourses of connecting and transgressing conceptually discreet entities, which eventually, much like migrant activism and Italian thought, solidify the gatekeeping that takes place on and in the borders of society. As I noted in Chapter 2, there exists a desperate upholding of the belief that alter-globalist activisms will save humanity and the planet. This book partakes in this desperation by conceptually 'globalising' acceleration as *the* problem. In terms of such globalisations emerging *as* alter-globalisation, we currently see this desperation being once more suppressed through constructing a higher-level narrative of 'clean' spaces and 'green' technologies as the next safe haven for justifiable transgressions and activities. I therefore continue my journey of deconstruction towards the next level of production that informs many alter-globalist practices in their unwanted quest to encapsulate the whole earth into its acceleration: climate change activism.

4   Humanism Overheating
The Conundrum of
Climate Change Activism

Whoever takes on the apocalyptic tone comes to signify to, if not tell, you something. What? The truth, of course.

>   Jacques Derrida, 'Of an Apocalyptic Tone' (53, 1992).

It is the *social itself* that, in contemporary discourse, is organized along the lines of a disaster-movie script.

>   Jean Baudrillard, *Simulacra and Simulation* (40, 1994).

Climate change is analogous to an attack from Mars, albeit in slow motion.

>   Paul G. Harris, *World Ethics and Climate Change* (189, 2010).

APOCALYPSE NOW?

Our deconstruction of activism is now starting to *gather speed*. It should be clear by now from the analyses in the previous chapters that the complicities of alter-globalist activisms tend to run through two entangled conceptual and technological problems. Firstly, by virtue of a naive use and imagination of new media as neutral or even utopian spaces for communication, these activisms are implicated in what I have termed 'speed-elitism.' Since speed-elitism is based on an accelerated technological and discursive mobilisation and dissimulation of the fundamental aporias of humanism— the productive tension between action and thought, as well as between the universality and the particularity of justice—it now appears that the democratic and emancipatory enterprises themselves engender speed and its ever-more-virulent forms of violence and exclusion. Secondly, since the rhetoric of connections, alliance, and crossing borders is an essential aspect of speed-elitism, exaltations of anything or anyone crossing borders like 'the migrant' as constituting some sort of new 'liberatory subjectivity' are ultimately misguided. This is true even if concern over the precarious conditions that actual refugees live in is surely called for. This suggests that neo-liberal acceleration points towards the limits of humanism, its subject-agent of liberation, and of *the critical project itself* insofar as this project has indeed become the basic ingredient for oppression. But this also suggests that the argument for the general dissolution of the subject into object-hood under neo-liberal globalisation and the extent to which 'humanity' has become its own target of exploitation and destruction, *qua apocalyptic argument*, directly exacerbates speed as well as humanist hope through reviving the critical project. Because the 'futural' aspect of left-wing activism and theorisation has produced its own concrete (real and material) problems, the limitations of humanism today directly solidify as 'real' contextual limitations to the contemporary exercise of 'freedom.' I argue in this final chapter on speed-elitist forms of activism that this in turn happens currently foremost through an increasing concern and obsession with the environment. This is also because the latter concern often complicates the straightforward humanist *border* between 'man' and 'nature' by being ambiguous about the source or origin of social change.

In this chapter, then, I suggest that the acceleration of the humanist aporia has currently found its apex in climate change activism, which is in many ways the hyper-modern enactment of earlier 80s and 90s environmentalist activism. In this sense, climate change activism inhabits an even more profound deconstruction than new media and no-border activism. This is essentially because its main assumption is that human activity is the *culprit* of our current ecological crisis, while simultaneously calling upon human action and debate to *avert* climate change. This paradox displays immediately that our era of technological acceleration affirms the hubristic image of the human subject-agent in its very attempt at critiquing human mastery of 'nature.' We will see that this paradoxical logic generates a highly mediated simulation of climate change in the media. This simulation is therefore not only profoundly 'real,' but also constitutes the perfect symptom as well as metaphor for our speed-elitist era and the reality of its fundamental instability. In effect, then, the trope of non-sustainability also projects into the near future an aspect of speed-elitism—emerging from the impossibility of complete humanist utopia that grounds the possibility of its political thought and action—that is already profoundly 'accidented,' to use Paul Virilio's phrasing.[1] The apocalyptic narrative of climate change is therefore not only what grounds this chapter's critique of climate change activism. It also opens up the factuality of climate change itself in order to envision not just alternative futures—precisely what such activism, in line with the spirit of new media and no-border politics, seeks to do as well. More importantly, since much activism and debate on the environment fails to deepen its questioning sufficiently in light of the exponentially raised stakes under speed-elitism, this envisioning must also generate an alternative reading of the present situation of climate change as a quintessentially politico-technological *apparition*.

Allow me to stress here that by calling climate change an 'apparition' I do not mean to say that the actual occurrence of climate change is simply false. To interpret the problematic of apparition in this way—that is, to oppose it to 'reality'—would be precisely the lazy misinterpretation many have also made of Baudrillard's conception of simulation.[2] Rather, the knee-jerk accusations hurled at those who are even modestly sceptical of climate change by immediately categorising such sceptics as being immoral right-wing capitalists are missing a central point: namely that many such sceptics are in fact fellow travellers in the larger environmentalist critique of modern science and technology that climate change activists seek to mount. After all, it is also my scepticism about the univocal virtue of new media and no-border activism that seeks to re-grasp activism's *spirit*. In other words, the simplistic division of the debate into 'for' or 'against' the truth or reality of climate change is not very helpful, and only serves to silence more complex analyses of the fundamental problems facing humanity today. This complication also entails the division between reality and representation, if only because technological acceleration has made media representation into the dominant reality. Climate change exists, which means that climate change is a simulation that signifies another even more urgent accident or catastrophe, which in turn means that currently popular climate change activism and thought are implicated in its mobilisation for speed-elitism due to the present-day enmeshment of simulation and acceleration. This chapter can then only start from the premise that the occurrence of anthropogenic climate change is true, as this would be the most *responsible* position; but it also acknowledges, in line with the argument laid out in Chapter 1, that as responsibilities go, they are always constituted in (or respond to) a wider historical and socio-economical imperative that finds its origins in Eucken's philosophy of activism. To overlay the duty of humanism to critique its own duty with the way responsible climate change activism finds its limitations in the truth-value of the climate change model is imperative in terms of understanding how radical alterity may emerge from the ambiguous ethics of speed. This imperative again points to the sheer force of neo-liberal globalisation and the mounting necessity to *urgently slow down*. In short, the humanist argument in climate change activism that criticises the inherent limitations of accelerating capitalist expansion due to its non-sustainability then directly constitutes this chapter's and this book's fundamental 'ecological' limitation.

This chapter will start its analysis of climate change activism by looking at the debates around the preservation of 'nature' and 'wilderness' in 80s and 90s traditional environmentalism, which also still continue today. Climate change activism is in many ways a reworking and an acceleration of the previous concerns of modern environmental activism in which I participated in my home university. Environmentalism, which was propelled into the public eye with the publication of Rachel Carson's *Silent Spring* in 1962, therefore provides a good starting point in order to discern which contradictory or paradoxical tropes and calls for action informed this earlier mode of 'green' political engagement. One of my arguments will namely be that, in its incessant compulsion to cover over its own internal contradictions, environmentalism has mutated into climate change activism due to the latter's heavy indebtedness to scientific and technological attempts at modelling 'reality' and making predictions. This analysis agrees partly with, for instance, Ulrich Beck's thesis on risk society in *World at Risk*, although it does not see the cosmopolitan impetus that arises from global risk as necessarily encouraging. Climate change as a techno-political apparition which is 'more real than reality itself' emerges out of the previous ghostly representation of 'nature' that was highly prevalent in environmentalism. It is here that the sheer force of technological reproduction and acceleration brings about the collapse of reality and representation in which the latter now outbids the former. This indiscernibility between the real and its description was, of course, as many post-structuralist theorists since Ludwig Wittgenstein have pointed out, always already the case;[3] but under the new conditions of speed, the artificial split between image and truth that has made possible modern science and philosophy since the onset of humanism now finally caves in onto itself. The analysis of the relationship between environmentalism and the media should therefore, I suggest, go way beyond more common descriptions in the social sciences of how the media influence popular opinion around climate change, although such analyses are certainly not without merit.[4] Once again, we will see that the illusion of noise-free, neutral, or transparent communication and representation allow for the possibility of climate science's truth-claims about 'nature,' even if such technological acceleration engenders increasing doubt and confusion regarding the truth of climate change and its causes, as well as to the appropriate moral response.[5] Such an increasing obsession with and confusion around climate change is also reminiscent of the general Cold War techno-logic of attraction and disorientation out of which new media emerged.[6]

Furthermore, as I already hinted at in Chapter 3, in the course of progressively more people effectively being swept up in the logic of speed by way of its material and discursive techniques of emancipation—that is, neo-liberal capitalism exhausting its market of 'humans'—activist attention shifts gradually to animals and 'nature' as the next romantic object. In terms of the continuation of the discourses typical to speed-elitism, the problematic romanticisation of the margins I bore out with my analyses of new media and no-border activism in Chapters 2 and 3 returns in environmental activism therefore firstly as the exaltation of nature and wilderness as being fundamentally outside of social institutions, as well as a call to 'go back to nature.' This exaltation leads then quite logically to the simulation of some kind of pristine 'nature' and 'wild' peoples in the media as a new object of a globalising nostalgia—a desire to become nature. The ghostly emergence in the media of and nostalgic longing for unspoiled nature, as the illusion of stable origin and identity, is hence akin to the rise of fundamentalisms I noted in Chapter 1. But simultaneously, the way environmentalism claims that assaults on nature are a direct assault on humanity also already complicates the distinction between the social (the human) and the natural. This makes possible the argument that terms like 'wilderness' and 'nature' may be somehow related to or gesture towards deconstruction by virtue of the undecidability of their status as being inside or outside the social. It also renders unstable the distinction between subject-agent and object-in-nature, as 'humanity' becomes both source and target of action and thought while the natural object seems to take its revenge.[7] Nonetheless, the rendering of 'nature' as an object of activist practice or method is immediately constitutive of the romantic idea of nature, which means that such an attempt to model or act on its destruction unintentionally obscures once more the very moment at which speed-elitism actually breaks down and shows itself to be illegitimate. 'Nature' and its preservation, in other words, cannot be enacted without landing oneself into a host of complications, just as much as deconstruction is not a method; to do so would simply reinforce speed-elitism and make such activism emerge as an effect of acceleration.

Of course, critiques of the ways in which 'nature' is and has been a social construction ever since the start of the romantic period in the West are numerous, and my aim is not to regurgitate all the intricacies of these illuminating critiques. My concern in this chapter is rather with how the very necessity of humanist thought and practices to defend nature from techno-science, as well as point out its construction by science, has today culminated in the global dissemination of the climate change model and its new forms of activism by virtue of techniques and technologies of speed. So while many in various environmental debates in the 90s worry about how post-modern interpretations around the social construction of 'nature' have rendered the ecological claim and its activisms moot, I instead want to point out that the post-modern interpretation has worked and still works hand in hand with the defence of the environment. This is because post-modernism gave birth to environmentalism's next generation of climate change activism *while* also magnifying the incredulity in environmentalist and climate change science. Moreover, it does so while also magnifying the incredulity towards the scientific project as such. I will illustrate this claim too when discussing some of the influential texts in the debate around nature and wilderness of academic intellectuals who are also environmental activists. We will see that in turn, out of the conundrum in which environmentalism finds itself, emerges a globalising compulsion in line with the imperialistic tendency in activism for which the climate change model lends itself very well indeed. Much of the ethical response to this globalising compulsion then starts to run through the call for a certain trans-nationalism and even cosmopolitanism, as in the work of Beck. We can also see this cosmopolitan moment emerging in the case of contemporary human-rights rhetoric. This cosmopolitanism, far from being the solution, marks the moment where national borders are required to be crossed for a new dissemination of the liberal idea of justice, and as such implicates itself in neo-liberal acceleration just as new media and migrant activisms do. The attempt at

rekindling civic engagement through climate change activism is hence reminiscent of and akin to the problems inherent to the idea of global human
rights, as both appear as symptoms of acceleration. Interestingly also, both
are quite in line with the alter-globalist 'think global act local' slogan. They
both also give the appearance of successfully tackling a problem while dissimulating fundamental inequalities related to their speed-elitist techniques
of enunciation. I therefore suggest that the politics of climate change also
constitute an instrument of risk management and population control, giving rise to new forms of global disciplining and commodification of which
the cosmopolitan imperative is but one aspect. In many ways, the climate
change model reworks once more certain Christian traits present in the
humanist endeavour, in which the updated narrative of 'our fall from para-
dise' engenders a sense of guilt and self-flagellation[8] that under conditions
of speed immediately calls for a hubristic 'we can fix this' techno-optimism
in order to foster more subjective activity and repress despair.[9] Finally,
then, climate change and climate change activism fundamentally appeal to
our basic experience as citizen-consumers under the era of speed as well as
co-construct that experience as a global one.

SAVING NATURE: ENVIRONMENTALISM
AND ITS DISCONTENTS

Academics and activists concerned with the demise and destruction of the
environment have tackled this issue in the last two decades from a myriad
of perspectives and in numerous ways, but there are two discernible tensions that one way or the other run through most of this work. The first of
these profound tensions is the attempt to align the critique of environmental destruction with a 'post-modern' critique of the modern interpretation
or representation of such an environment. The second bafflement, related
to the first one in ways I will explain shortly, concerns the issue of how the
drive to solve or fix the assault on the natural environment cannot help
but be mobilized through those discourses and techniques that themselves
stand at the basis of that assault. Allow me to explain a bit more in depth
this impulse to 'save nature' and its complicity in the techniques and economy of acceleration by now likening such an attempt more closely than I
did in Chapter 2 to what Derrida calls the 'archive fever' that, like a sort of
modern disease, suffuses increasingly all aspects of society today. This fever
started with the modern museumisation of exotic peoples, runs through
the encapsulation of radical alterity in new media and no-border activism, and culminates in an urgency under hyper-modern conditions that
becomes self-defeating.[10] As I suggested, the real tragedy of the assault on
and the disappearances of wilderness and nature calls forward a thoroughly
ethical activist-scientific desire to prevent this from happening by using
the immense possibilities of contemporary media, military, and scientific

technologies. But ironically, it is precisely the use of these technologies and their economic arrangements that had caused (and still causes) the gradual *extinction* of nature in the first place. This is because the activist-scientific quest to rescue 'nature' from going extinct due to ongoing exploitative capitalist processes erroneously assumes that nature is a *pre-given static entity* that can then be simply salvaged, returned to, or stored.

This experience or image of nature as 'static'—one we see returning in the general debate in the social sciences around the assumption that social construction suggests changeability and being natural does not—is hence a techno-linguistic illusion. This static depiction of nature therefore falls in the now familiar traps of seeing new media and archiving technologies as neutral tools as well as of assuming that the ideology and institutional practices behind the desire to 'archive' and represent are universal. But since the technicity of archiving at its basis is one that is already entangled with the dominant culture that archives, the recognition of what counts as 'nature' today has as its logical parameters speed-elitist *culture*. Once again, we can see that the well-intended activist attempt to 'salvage otherness' from the tragedy of disappearance under globalisation works completely *in accordance with* that very tragedy, just as new media activism and migrant activism does. Importantly, the general ideology of speed-elitism, grounded as it is in humanism, relies primarily on the artificial distinction between culture and nature (or humans and their environment) and in turn increasingly sets this false distinction to work for capitalist reproduction. I suggest that Derrida calls this merger between the archiving of nature and capitalist reproduction in *Monolingualism of the Other* a 'truly tragic economy' (30) not simply because 'nature' suffers tragically from human culture—eventually, after all, human culture is arguably also 'nature,' which means nature remains one way or the other, even if actual species may sadly go extinct—but because of two other facets of the quest to and for its salvation. Firstly, it is tragic because this attempt at rescuing has already failed from its very inception (or, in fact, *due to* its very inception). Secondly, it is subsequently tragic because this immediate failure is reminiscent and representative of our own mortality and the limitations of our very own being or practice—our own 'tragic' existence that we tried so hard to overcome. The quest to save 'nature' is therefore nothing less than a dissimulation of the general failure of modern culture to come to grips with its own limits and the event of death, yet at the same time inhabits the lure of true radical alterity that such a taboo on showing limitations also generates. This acknowledgement of the final unknowability of such radical alterity, as well as the diminishing diversity of species on the planet while attempting to 'archive' them in the media and nature reserves, is of course in turn a profanity in the face of the overall democratic endeavour. The argument that these events entail a profound immorality is then not some universal ethics that emerges spontaneously from nature, but a projection of the humanist aporia which presents itself in environmentalist thought as a *mise-en-abyme* in need of covering over in order to keep the scientific and democratic dream alive. This covering over runs incessantly, as we will see, through the technological reinstatement of the activist subject-agent and the wider narrative of emancipation in the service of speed-elitism. The problems of the environment and their technical solutions then generate a sensation of a humanity 'running towards its own death,' which may very well be an accurate estimation—or at least, that is what this chapter responsibly affirms.

We can see the above bafflements very much at work in environmental discussions in the 80s and 90s. One of the major texts in the humanities that started the critique of 'nature' and especially 'wilderness' as a social construction is William Cronon's 'The Trouble with Wilderness.' Cronon adeptly connects the romantic call to preserve 'wilderness' to forms of racism and sexism, like the idea of nature as 'feminine' and 'primitive,' correctly showing that the notion 'serves as the unexamined foundation on which so many of the quasi-religious values of environmentalism rest' (14, 10). Modern environmentalism then exhibits for Cronon a form of anthropocentric hubris because it assumes that humanity can destroy as well as rescue wilderness. Nonetheless, Cronon suggests at the end of his piece that the idea of the 'wild' has some merit since it also exactly signifies that which is beyond human control, thereby reinstating the environmentalist endeavour (19). I argue that it is precisely the indeterminability of whether the 'wild' or 'nature' is inside or outside culture that allows for Cronon to make an appeal to a *real* wilderness, which in turn salvages the scientific and humanist quest of our or its emancipation. However, the split between complicit and real wilderness is eventually an artificial distinction, whose semiotic difference *itself* today becomes implicated in an accelerated technological reproduction. It is by virtue of the ambiguity of the status of the term that Cronon can enact the 'conjuring trick' of giving environmentalism its politics back, thereby remaining faithful to the institution of activism and all its complicities I outlined in Chapter 1. Whatever exactly the 'post-modern' impetus that informs Cronon's critique, it clearly shows that this impetus is, far from being politically relativistic, rather a moment that allows for a political re-enablement. We could perhaps then say that in the case of environmentalist politics, a mere constructionist critique does not go far enough to unsettle the general logic of activism, because such activism *as well as its critique* has run headlong into its own ecological and linguistic limits. This is the general form activist thought takes on the level of its argument as part of what scholars like Ulrich Beck would call 'reflexive modernisation.'[11]

Other prominent pieces by environmental scholars, like Kate Soper's fittingly titled 'Nature/"nature" ' and Kevin DeLuca's 'A Wilderness Environmentalism Manifesto,' enact the same curious logic, albeit in different ways. DeLuca's text is in particular interesting because it rather candidly displays the near madness that underlies the environmentalist project—and let me again stress here that I do not mean to say that this madness makes this project illegitimate; far from it. Rather, this madness marks the absurdity of our constant technologically informed shuttling between hope and despair under the intensified politics of humanism. Making a stab at the Greek philosopher Protagoras, DeLuca claims that environmentalism can and should be done as a 'wilderness environmentalism, wherein wilderness is the measure of all things,' rather than humans as the measure of all things (40). But as I already noted above, there is in the final analysis no ethics that emerges from nature as such, which means that DeLuca can only make such an argument by virtue of the human-centred ethics that inspired environmentalism in the first place. His earlier points about simply preserving forests no matter the human interests in using or altering them appear to the average reader as shockingly unjustified. This requires that DeLuca eventually, of course, makes a case that environmentalism is (and should be) beneficial to humanity *at large* by arguing that 'caring for wilderness *is* caring for people' (43). The enactment of his humanist responsibility therefore compels him full circle back to where he started, away from the 'mad' yet logical claim that the priority should no longer be firstly caring for people. In many ways, DeLuca's narrative mirrors the deconstruction that inhabits the 'irrational rationality' typical of speed-elitism.[12] As I have shown in Chapter 1, once again the claim from the margins turns out to be a claim from the centre. But importantly also, DeLuca's re-enunciation of the humanist trope makes this circular logic consistent with an increasingly global conception of humanity due to its universalising gesture. This global conception results in the trope becoming excellent fodder for capitalist expansion. It is out of the latter tension that climate change activism will get born.

Kate Soper's article on the distinction between the construction and representation of nature, and the 'real' nature that environmentalism requires in order to justify its activism, is likewise fascinating in terms of how its argument relates to the formal enunciation and in turn to the mode of production of that argument. In order to elucidate the exemplary status of Soper's critique and affirmation of nature in the larger ecological debate, I will at this juncture connect my conceptualisation of speed-elitism to what I see as Jean Baudrillard's cardinal point throughout his later oeuvre, which has also been wrongly dismissed by many critics as typical of 'relativistic' or 'nihilistic' post-structuralist or post-modern theory. Increasingly all forms of politics, as I argued in Chapter 2 by way of Jodi Dean's work, find themselves wrapped up in a neo-liberal logic that relies on the collapse of the semiotic—the realm of representation and signification—into the realm of capital relations, by virtue of neo-liberal globalisation relying on maximising transactions. Baudrillard likewise argues in 'The Mirror of Production' that this collapse has become possible because the axiomatic (the realm of capital relations) has come to rely on the incessant mediation of signs through the consumption of the differentiation between signs (105–106). New media in particular facilitate this logic because they allow for the incessant circulation, multiplication, and differentiation of signs. Signs become objects for consumption, and difference merely sustains the exploitation of the conceptual fallacy of pure binary oppositions for economic growth, just as I explained in Chapter 1 with my critique on Jordan. So what Baudrillard aims at is that the conceptual split in Saussurean semiotics of the sign into signifier and signified (like Soper's nature/Nature) constitutes not a universal truth about the generation of meaning, but marks a historically specific moment in this later stage of capitalism. The concept of the signified emerges alongside the capitalist model of exchange value as a supposed derivative of use value, but use value in the form of so-called 'real' desires, just like the signified or the referent, is simply conjured up as an 'alibi,' as Baudrillard cheekily calls it in 'For a Critique of the Political Economy of the Sign' (78), for a capitalism that justifies itself by relying on the assumption that those desires for emancipation or salvation are natural. Humanism therefore once more appears in activisms that seek salvation (of nature, for instance) as the grounding ideology of speed-elitism by virtue of the unquestionable status of the subject-agent of liberation. But this anthropocentrism at its heart *is* also the problem of anthropogenic environmental pollution.

This way in which the solution is the problem shows itself in Soper's article in the way she ultimately keeps the spirit of ecological justice going. The moment where Soper responsibly discerns between 'nature' as an image tainted by anthropocentric politics and 'adequately' represented nature (30) worth fighting for, so as to keep the vision of ecological justice alive, marks, I claim, exactly the point at which this opposition enters the realm of capital circulation. This entrance into circulation happens by virtue of the energy-consuming typesetting, printing, and dissemination of the book in which her chapter is included, but also by virtue of the assumption of a distinction between discourses closer to and further away from reality that informs her argument. The *desire* for finding a language closer to 'real nature,' one that revives the environmentalist duty, is after all one that is much more in line with the demands of speed-elitism for an 'alibi' for activism than the acknowledgement of its social construction. Or rather, one could say that the analysis of 'nature' as social construction cries out for a politics around 'real nature' to cover over the abyss of speed. Nonetheless, this play of 'nature' between sign and object in her piece results temporarily in a sensation of activist vertigo; 'nature' becomes indeed that sign at which the anthropocentric logic of humanism starts to crumble. Soper's piece hence unwittingly demonstrates the aporia of humanism—its autoimmunity or deconstruction—by showing that the post-modern critique on the construction of the term 'nature' in environmentalism follows from an *ecological* demand regarding its limitations.

I am calling the above sensation one gets by reading Soper's piece a feeling of 'activist vertigo' because there occurs a terrified suspension of the self-righteous activist movement forward, as if one—to use a metaphor from nature—stares down an enormous overhang into a ravine. This deep-seated terror is, I suggest, quite literally the fear of emptiness or death that activist and academic subjects must feel as being inappropriate due to the neo-liberal demand for activity of the subject-agent. The fear of 'not doing' therefore today generates a stronger fear of death in late-capitalist cultures, even if dying itself is increasingly relegated to specialist settings, and even if it was perhaps initially the fear of death that gave rise to the humanist discourses of emancipation and (Christian) salvation. 'Nature' becomes in this outlook the ultimate object for technological mastery, but equally the ultimate agent of revenge and destruction by way of its channelling such mastery back onto the human subject as target—or so it *appears* to us in any case. What really happens is rather a pervasive redistribution of actual death and dying at the hands of the neo-liberal machine, in which the speed-elite emerges as the winners in terms of what one calls 'life-expectancy'—a fittingly statisticist and managerial expression of which the resultant linguistic ambiguity of 'nature' is only symptomatic.[13] We will see this bizarre appearance and circularity of the lethal accident return in climate change activism later.

As a final analysis of 90s environmentalist thought for now, I want to focus briefly on this 'vertigo,' which Bronislaw Szerszynski designates as a sensation of 'not knowing what to do' in 'On Knowing What to Do.' Szerszynski's chapter title is obviously reminiscent of my point in Chapter 1 about the productive tension between activism and theory by acknowledging immediately the 'knowing' that environmentalist 'doing' must rely on, and vice versa. Most of the chapter comprises an astute critique of the various scientific and romantic interpretations of 'nature' and the ecological politics derived from the interpretations, which he accurately traces back into the problem of the necessity of representation of origins and realities. This critique of the construction of the 'real' and our claims according to Szerszynski lead up to an activist impasse as we now, after the post-modern critique on environmentalism, no longer 'know what to do.' But Szerszynski eventually cannot leave the reader hanging with this 'bleak narrative' which he claims he only mounted to 'emphasise the depth and complexity of the predicament' (130). In order to fill the void opened up by the deconstruction of 'nature,' he immediately seeks rescue in foregrounding once more the idea of human ability and thinking, which today ought to have us 'rethink the human' (131–132). Only when this reflection is properly begun, we might, says he, 'begin to see what it might *really* mean for ecology to tell us what to do' (133, emphasis in original). Being 'told what to do,' therefore, I suggest, emerges from his narrative as being subjected to (or the subject of) the humanist imperative of questioning eventually also the human. This self-questioning has nothing to do with 'nature' as such (whatever that is), but rather with the technical and epistemological conditions for self-reflection within hyper-modernity that situate Szerszynski's argument firmly within an aesthetic of acceleration.

Out of this aesthetic, nature appears as a reality (however ghostly) urging us into moral action, and 'post-modernist ideas of language-as-free-play' (132) appear as the socio-cultural negative of nature. Post-structuralist analysis becomes, in Szerszynski's text, once more the scapegoat of the ineffectuality and perplexity of the activist predicament under acceleration. But post-structuralism instead, as I claimed in Chapter 1, rather offers a way of mirroring with a difference that very predicament. With this in mind, I will now turn to the politics around the pressing issue of climate change and the ways it inhabits a globalisation of these ecological and activist concerns.

A CLIMATE OF TOO MUCH CHANGE

As Gabriel Ignatow also writes in *Transnational Identity Politics and the Environment*, the traditional environmentalism of the 80s and 90s quickly 'lost its avant-garde status and its universalising ambitions' (117). According to Ignatow, environmentalism lost its appeal because of the post-modern context in which it was usurped, as post-modernism eschewed all scientific truth claims and hence also those engendered by works of science like Carson's *Silent Spring*. However, I suggest that Ignatow's account does not do justice to the complexities of the environmental debate under the hypermodern conditions of speed-elitism of which such post-modernism appears only as its aesthetic effect. So while Ignatow's account agrees with mine in that it is not post-modern theory that caused the environmental impasse, he tends nevertheless to understand post-modernity only as a social condition. I instead argue that the complication I sketched above that arises in environmentalism, due to its indebtedness to the aporia of humanism, has propelled the seed that was planted in the collective unconscious of the advanced industrialised societies of the image of the 'man-made natural disaster' forward into the spectre of global climate change. This propelling shows itself partly in the shift some environmentalism makes towards trans-national eco-identity politics that Ignatow describes, but more so in the highly mediatised scientific debates about global warming and the incessant managerial attempts at solutions like geo-engineering, didactic movies and video-games, and green derivatives trading.

These technological and managerial solutions, however, do nothing to subvert the speed-elitist system and ideology that underlie the problem of climate change, as they do not go far enough in challenging speed-elitism's fundamental assumptions and techniques. This means that the activist promise of the future absolution by way of humanist-scientific thought from the future threat of global warming immediately aggravates disenfranchisement and pollution *now*. Let me illustrate this by first briefly analysing a widely used educational game designed to combat climate change called *Global Warming Interactive—CO2Fx*. This web-based game, funded by the United States National Science Foundation and developed by environmentalists from a range of American consultancies and educational organisations, aims at teaching secondary-school students the sorts of decision making involved in global warming. The game invariably starts with a map of the country of Brazil in the 1960s, and gives statistics about the carbon emission, air temperature, and general welfare of the population. The player can control government budget expenditures for science, agriculture, social services, and development initiatives, after which the game timeline jumps ten years into the future, generating results based on these expenditures. The game ends by showing the relative increase in temperature in the virtual year of 2060, warning the player that more international cooperation is required to really tackle global warming.

The problem with *Global Warming Interactive* is that it completely obscures the relationship between the computing technology that sustains the *CO2Fx* simulation and the reality of climate change. A telling moment of this dissimulation is when the game urges the player to 'switch off the television!' while the energy consumption involved in the infrastructure, mode of production and dissemination, student use, and tools that sustain the game itself is blissfully ignored. If one wants to seriously reduce consumption, the game should not have been played or even produced at all. The game also oversimplifies how government decisions affect a complex issue like climate change, and is fraught with problematic and often techno-utopian assumptions about how to tackle climate change. A good example of this is the recurring recommendation throughout the game to the player to spend more money on scientific research, as this expenditure will supposedly solve or alleviate global warming. The speed-elitist, humanist, and techno-utopian discourses that permeate American academia and consultancy firms are clearly reflected in *Global Warming Interactive*, inculcating the student with a set of beliefs that lies precisely at the base of current environmental pollution. Ironically, it is this speed-elitist system of beliefs and techniques that in turn causes the kinds of economical disenfranchisement that urges certain groups of poor people in a country like Brazil to survive on environmentally unfriendly business solutions, like slash-burning the forests. One is also left to wonder why the game uses Brazil in the first place, and not the United States—arguably the largest global polluter today. There is indeed a problematic neo-colonialist undertone to the one-country version of *Global Warming Interactive*. Extending the content of the game by including more countries in the simulation, as the developers seek to do, would not assuage this problem, but would concur with the contemporary shift from previous colonialist to speed-elitist hierarchies by way of a global encapsulation. By giving the player simulated governmental omnipotence through the 'archiving' of the economical and social structures underlying global warming in that 'other' country of Brazil, the player gets the illusion of dealing constructively with the major 'accident' of climate change and its impact on threatened peoples while actually fuelling it. Meanwhile, player or student empathy and activity are displaced into the instantaneous networks of ever increasing neo-liberal circulation and production.

The illusion of constructive engagement with the pressing climate change issue through seemingly 'clean' and 'neutral' technologies, together with the distancing effect brought about by these technologies from their social and environmental implications, make the student and activist unwittingly complicit in the globalising neo-liberal endeavour. The same goes for the recent spate of 'climate change apps' like *Greenmeter* and *GreenYou* for iPhone, as well as the various global 'climate app contests' set up by the United Nations and the World Bank. Environmental salvation is in these applications always just around the corner. The World Bank contest, for instance, states in full speed-elitist fashion that 'Access to freely available climate-related data is essential to catalyze the changes in policies, investments and technologies that will be needed if we are to move towards a climate-smart future.' But all such applications and contests really do is producing globally networked flows and reproducing the mirage of the human participant-consumer-activist at the centre of revolutionary change through her or his *technè*. So despite, or rather again because of, the good intentions of the activists and educators who built such applications, these games exhibit a virtualisation of thought and action under neo-liberal globalisation and its speed-elitist modes of intensified inclusion and exclusion. These games can therefore be understood as attempts at (eventually unsuccessfully) managing and containing the 'accident of the real' brought about by the technologies of speed. What is even more worrisome is that the very attempt to raise awareness about climate change—the unveiling of the 'real' problem underlying globalisation today—results in the intensified capitalist circulation of 'the real' *as sign* in the media, just as Baudrillard also suggests.

I am using this minor example of a didactic video game here to illustrate the extent to which the political and managerial attempts at combating climate change themselves follow the representational and aesthetic logic of the mass and new media. So while *CO2Fx* is arguably 'just a game' with artificially set parameters, the very same logic of simulation operates on the scale of global politics by means of the apocalyptic staging and subsequent economical, scientific, and technical propositions. Moreover, the activist argument that requires the justification of these propositions and attempts by signifying the 'real' problem, like 'nature' with earlier environmental politics, renders such activism *as well as my deconstructivist book* complicit in speed-elitism by virtue of their promissory status and apocalyptic narrative. Contra, for instance, the claim by Erik Swyngedouw in 'Apocalypse Forever?' that the climate change model signals the post-political moment (215), I suggest that it is by reworking the apocalyptic narrative present in the environmental imperative through climate change activism and its affirmation of the underlying assumptions of global warming that results in the intensification of politics on which speed-elitism thrives. I hence do not agree with Swyngedouw that 'apocalyptic imaginations are decidedly populist and foreclose proper political framing' (219), because within these imaginaries resides also the critique of a monstrous capitalism that Swyngedouw so astutely retrieves. So whereas the climate change model and its current 'solutions' decidedly reflect the neo-liberal status quo, I would hesitate to suggest that climate change is a *deliberate* governmental or corporate ploy to rule by means of fear so as to better exploit citizen-consumers, although government and industry certainly have stepped onto the greenhouse bandwagon to expand the futures and derivatives market and to sell 'green' products and incentives. Rather, at issue is the politics of acceleration behind the construction of reality by means of the discursive and material techniques of visualisation and dissimulation.

The one profound dissimulation that complicates much present-day online climate-change activism is the extent to which web-hosting and traffic aggravates environmental pollution and oil depletion. Especially large server parks, Internet backbones and routers, and park coolers require considerable and constant amounts of energy.[14] As with *CO2Fx*, this amount of pollution, which disproportionately puts disenfranchised communities and peoples at risk, gets dissimulated by way of the aesthetically pleasing and smooth surface of climate-change activism's websites. Much of this aestheticisation is done on activist websites like One Blue Marble through lean black-on-white fonts and images of pristine nature or endangered animals, of which the tree and the polar bear are the prime poster children. As I have argued above, it appears from these websites that the desire to archive 'nature' runs in concordance with the factual disappearance of that very bit of 'nature.' The websites pretend to communicate in 'noise-free' fashion what is really the nostalgic desire for and ubiquitous consumption of a lost past. Besides this nostalgic and pristine visual representation of 'nature' on such websites, much of the discursive techniques reflect a similar romantic, anthropomorphised, and often feminine conception of nature. The 'Climate Justice Assembly Declaration' from Friends of the Earth, for instance, reads that 'the Earth is saying "enough"!' while calling for a day of global action in defence of 'Mother Earth.' This feminisation of nature—leading to the twin representations of nature as either an ideal site or a demonic force—is of course nothing new in itself. But what is new today is how the call for global activism is predicated on a trans-border imaginary evoked by the 'one earth' that climate change inhabits. The romantic idea of a mother earth under siege allows for a globalisation of struggles quite akin to how the 'migrant' comes to represent the global speed-elitist imagination in Chapter 3. The logical result is once more, as we also saw in Chapters 2 and 3, a strong emphasis on forging alliances globally; the 'Climate Justice Assembly Declaration' stresses that 'We need to globalize these solutions,' whereas the Environmental Justice and Climate Change Initiative (EJCC) claims in 'A Climate of Change' that 'Ultimately, accomplishing climate justice will require that new alliances are forged and traditional movements

are transformed' (1). EJCC, in addition, advocates in their mission statement, called 'What we believe,' to use 'the power of the Internet to . . .
mobilize forces for action.' Both documents, however, do not discuss this
mobilisation through oil-devouring new media, and remain silent about
exactly which kinds of alliances and connections need to be built.

This silence on the matter of what kinds of alliances and with whom
is, I suggest, no mere coincidence. Neither is the shift in the rhetoric from
environmental activism to the importance of climate *justice* without signifi-
cance. As we saw with the discussion of DeLuca's piece, one of the tensions
in earlier environmental activism resides in the way the claim for some pure
'nature' always ends up running through humanist ideas of salvation—there
is no ethics that emerges from nature as such. The reworking of this tension
in climate change activism leads to a tendentious welding together of racial,
class-based, and gendered struggles with the environmental cause by way
of the universal 'one earth' rhetoric. As in the problematic encapsulation
of a variety of struggles under the umbrella of 'the multitude' in Hardt and
Negri's *Empire*, recent climate-justice discourse posits the global-warming
issue as containing within itself all alter-globalist efforts. The EJCC document, for example, states that 'all justice is climate justice' (1) and that
'racism causes bad climate policy' (3) by pointing out the statistical relationship between being non-white or poor and being affected by environmental hazards. Friends of the Earth even ventures to say that 'the struggles
for climate justice and social justice are one and the same.' But while it is
one thing to quite correctly point out relationships between marginalisation and pollution, it is quite another to claim that climate activism itself
will alleviate or annul all other forms of oppression. Worse even, the latter
document eventually works firmly within the current economical frame by
sympathetically suggesting that 'the economies of low-income communities' need to be 'strengthen[ed]' (1). This should be done by creating a global
legal sphere that allows for a calculation of leakage of carbon emissions
across borders and the development of 'green technologies' which should
be 'exported to developing nations' so as to spur their improvement (4).
However well-meant, all this is very much in step with the general impetus
of neo-liberal globalisation. It fails to think through how the very rhetoric
of the dissolution of borders, technological development, and the 'bring-
ing up to speed' of marginalised groups is in fact intimately connected to
the aggravation of poverty and climate change itself. The abstraction of
alliances is therefore the marker of the violence of actual globalisation, as
it washes out the profound contradictions and opposing aims of various
forms of struggles.

The narrative on the activist website One Blue Marble exemplifies this
utter failure to connect climate change to the 'accidents' of the neo-liberal
economy best. The opening statement on its glossy website, hosted at the
Point In Space server park in the United States, reads in dramatic fashion

The financial crisis? Bah! That was the pesky little villain the hero-ine dispatched in the opening scene just to show you that she really is something fierce. Truth to tell, the financial crisis is a mosquito. . . . Climate change will devastate our new world economy. . . . If this was a Hollywood blockbuster, the clock would be ticking off the last 10 seconds as the sweat-spattered heroine makes the ultimate decision . . . Cut the red wire or the green one . . . as the fate of humanity hangs in the balance.

One Blue Marble advises the development of 'clean technologies' in order to save this world economy and to 'provide a better standard of life in the developing world and alleviate the most pressing issues of poverty.' It even sells polyester-containing sweatshirts and bumper stickers in its online store to disseminate this message. Once more, this is all very much in line with speed-elitist discourse. But more interesting than this overt techno-push (and not unrelated) is the cinematic image the website invokes of an apocalyptic action movie, with an appeal to the truth of an environmental disaster 'out there' quite similar to Al Gore's *An Inconvenient Truth*.[15] I argue that the disaster movie, as likewise reflected in the quote from Bau-drillard at the beginning of this chapter, is today the sublimated repre-sentation of the socio-economic unconscious desperation under neo-liberal acceleration. I suggest in turn that One Blue Marble's action-heroine script attempts to recuperate the anthropocentric techno-optimism that a mere disaster movie actually ending in catastrophe might threaten to dismantle. The punch line that 'We need a Star Trekian future' on the website is telling here. This is because *Star Trek* indeed represents the quintessential human-ist and scientific utopian endeavour by way of film and television technol-ogy.[16] The whole tone of mobilisation for a war of all citizens-consumers is eerily reminiscent of the historical backdrop of film- and new media tech-nologies themselves, which were, of course, developed in conjunction with propagandistic and otherwise intensified war efforts during the two world wars and the Cold War. The shuttling movement or tension between des-peration and techno-optimism in speed-elitist society—a shuttling between optimism and panic we also see in the contemporary stock exchange—is hence well expressed in the standard narrative arc of the disaster and action movie that One Blue Marble appropriates. In all cases, moreover, technol-ogy manages to save the day: at the stock exchange through trades and futures calculations, and in light of climate change through the proposition of 'clean and green' technologies. Eventually, though, this suppression of fear can only lead to more (fear of) accidents.

We can gather from these activist depictions that the climate change model functions as some sort of synthetic mirror to humanity; it reflects back to us 'as truth' the pervasive scientific and humanist fantasies under speed-elitism—those of the elimination of noise, of equality for all, and of complete emancipation—while simultaneously questioning these fantasies' validity. All this must be understood in light of the scientific and humanist models themselves harbouring these elements already by way of their grounding assumptions, which our technological and media apparatuses then merely reconstruct, disseminate, and inflate as if it were reality. This reality-effect works through these technologies in their ability to provide us with the appropriate data like infrared satellite images which show higher temperatures in certain geographical areas, or extrapolations of ecological change into the near future. *Skeptical Science,* an iPhone app made by an Australian environmental physicist, even near-automates the superficial 'for' and 'against' of the climate debate by way of presenting quotations from 'real' climate data explanations, so that the user can 'just point at [her] phone the next time someone argues against climate change.'[17] This application not only exemplifies the ongoing virtualisation of thought and debate for capital flows, but more seriously mirrors back to its user the illusion of direct access and influence on the truth of climate change. I suggest that it is this techno-mirroring—the *allegorical* function of the model that renders us part of an imaginary cosmopolitan community—that has made this particular scientific model so fashionable and popular, and not its bare scientific legitimacy. Despite One Blue Marble's insistence that now all real scientists agree that global warming is a scientific fact, such consensus within the scientific community may very well be the 'tyranny of the majority' that operates in projects like Indymedia as well.

ENVIRONMENTALISM'S COSMOPOLITAN MOMENT

The globalisation of struggles that climate change activism calls for, and the ways in which it justifies this call through a rhetoric of rights for humans and 'nature,' segues quite logically into a cosmopolitan political imagination. I argue that the promising idea of cosmopolitanism, far from being innocent, should instead urge us to think through those forces that give this concept and its utopian trans-national imagination its contemporary momentum, always keeping in mind that it is its promissory status that implicates it in acceleration. In Chapter 3, I discussed how the migrant functions as a symbol of radical alterity for the speed-elite due to these migrants' supposed inherent contestation of all national and otherwise stratifying borders. Sandro Mezzadra and Fabio Raimondi in 'Van mondiale beweging naar multitude' went so far as to suggest that the 'new subjectivities' of migrants are exemplary of the 'new cosmopolitan demands for freedom' (2). While ignoring the global inter-connectedness of contemporary forms of violence and disenfranchisement may certainly be remedied with an appeal to a cosmopolitan legal architecture as Mezzadra and Raimondi do, I argue that the latter nonetheless more often than not encompasses the globalisation of an ethics of rights and freedom that is fundamental to speed-elitism.

The ways in which radical Italian thought heralds the crossing of borders returns forcefully in the climate-change-activist debate through its quintessential cosmopolitan imaginary. As the One Blue Marble website also dutifully proclaims, 'Climate change is a matter for all humanity.' In many ways, climate change activism in fact *allows* for this cosmopolitan argument to be put forward. Such activism therefore implicates itself in the globalisation of a speed-elitist imaginary when simultaneously arguing for a global remedy against climate change. As a last excursion into the intensification of the humanist aporia that finds its apex in climate activism, I claim that the cosmopolitan moment is hence not merely a fortunate by-product of 'risk society,' as Ulrich Beck would have it, but is shaped by the demands of acceleration.

A good example of the way in which cosmopolitanism emerges as a normative solution against climate change in line with speed-elitism is eminent environmental ethics professor Paul Harris' *World Ethics and Climate Change*. Harris quite rightly points to the problem of the increase in affluent consumerism everywhere (and not just the West) for the crisis of environmental non-sustainability. In this sense, Harris's claim parallels my argument about speed-elitism being an exponent and a displacement of previous forms of privilege into other parts of the networked globe. But the prescriptive 'world ethics' that Harris recommends as the new cosmopolitan moment is solely based on a utilitarian notion of individual human rights that must transcend national borders. Such a 'globalisation of justice' (184) through an appeal to individual responsibility and action fails to connect the ways in which such humanist and Eurocentric discourse has fuelled capital acceleration, which in turn spurs global warming. Harris even wants this cosmopolitanism to engage 'distant and future peoples' (185) in order to accumulate climate action in ways reminiscent of the general encapsulation of alterity under ever-expanding neo-liberal capitalism. The call for individual responsibility to lessen consumption does nothing to tackle the root cause of climate change, but simply assigns such individuals their cosmopolitan status without the insurrection of a supra-national space of politics. Hence the space for the human subject-agent individualism that grounds speed-elitism gets enlarged. It also becomes clear from the above that the argument for the curtailing of climate change may be very well opposed to the demand for global justice in terms of the eradication of poverty; if the only means to escape poverty or annihilation today is to jump on the speed-elitist bandwagon, then denying such acceleration for the sake of the environment may amount to death for some. This is once again the extremely aporetic situation that the humanist and activist endeavour finds itself in. 'Climate justice' at times does and at times does not equal other forms of justice, despite the aforementioned activist projects lumping them so eagerly together. As I proposed at the end of Chapter 1, the problem of as well as the appeal to *justice* appears here once more to reside at the heart of contemporary acceleration.

It is for this reason of normative and prescriptive cosmopolitan ethics being tainted with 'elitism, imperialism and capitalism' that Beck in *World at Risk* seeks to distinguish between such an 'impure' and a more narrowly defined unanticipated cosmopolitanism that 'befalls us' as part of world risk society (61). Beck makes an astute analysis in *World at Risk* that points out how climate change is indeed representative of the 'dynamic of world risk society' (81). As I too have argued, Beck suggests that the covering up or dramatisation of risk results in a politics of anticipation, exemplified by apocalyptic narratives and debatable scientific models that are thoroughly implicated in the financial and military globalisation by means of the 'futural' pre-emptive strike. The future risk of climate change, according to Beck, precisely generates the urge for cosmopolitanism in that it 'prompts us to make new beginnings that overcome boundaries' (61). But Beck forgets that any such political and environmental activism is itself also part and parcel of the 'futural' aspect of economistic risk calculation. My concern with Beck's analysis would hence be that one cannot so easily split the normative or negative from the positive or affirmative impetus of cosmopolitanism, as the demand 'to make new beginnings' *is itself also already a tainted demand* that seeks to be responsible to the humanist activist quest. The particularity of that demand shows itself in the argument to 'overcome boundaries' quite typical of speed-elitism. Beck is then quite right in calling global risk society one of 'enforced enlightenment' because the acknowledgement of risks like global warming functions as a catalyst for new global alliances and a revival of Enlightenment ideals. However, all these in turn spark the attempt at calculating and managing risk that Beck himself also performs by way of theoretically extrapolating a 'good' cosmopolitanism and fostering active 'transformation' vis-à-vis widespread denial and the 'apathy of post-modern nihilism' (48). I am not suggesting, however, that Beck is unaware of the complicity of cosmopolitanism in global capitalism, but that the conundrum he lands himself in shows that the ethics of world risk society seem to fall apart at the very moment they seek to globalise its constitutive formal structures and discourses of acceleration.

If the blanket incorporation of all of humanity into the cosmopolitan battle against climate change marks the limits of humanism insofar as it runs out of humans to include, the shift towards rescuing nature or the earth shows the point at which humanism tips over and falls back into itself. At issue is therefore finally what the transformation of neo-liberal capitalism really has in store, if not simply the ongoing usurpation of all 'natural' beings into the speed-elitist machinery. One final example of how this happens in climate-change activism is the proposal for the Universal Declaration of the Rights of Mother Earth, drawn up by a wealth of environmental activists from all over the world during a conference in Bolivia. The well-meant proposal has all the indications of a certain profound desperation—like a final sigh of unwilling surrender emanating from its four bold articles on 'the rights of mother earth.' This sense of desperation is not surprising considering that in Bolivia global warming has allegedly caused some glaciers to melt, in turn resulting in a lack of clean water for two major cities—another disaster-movie script come alive. The proposal starts with the opening statement that 'Mother Earth is a living being' (1). It further states that 'she' has the right to 'continue its vital cycles free from human disruptions' as well as her 'right to integral health' (2). The initial charming naivety of the proposal, and the way it plays out the problematic image of the feminine as 'nurturing' that we also saw with early environmentalism, is also a function of the relativistic and romantic status it grants to other 'beings,' which include 'ecosystems, natural communities, species and all natural entities' (3). This inclusion of mother earth as a caring 'living being' nonetheless runs through yet another oppressive homogenization of various struggles worldwide against coercion and pollution, forcing them into a supposed commensurability through humanist and liberal ideas of justice and inter-cultural dialogue. Bolivian activist Evo Morales's words in an interview with Naomi Klein that 'we need to recover the values of the indigenous people' indeed likewise assumes that these peoples are or were all equally environmentally friendly *in the modern sense*, and that modern global democracy can 'recuperate' such lost values. But the method of recuperation integrates such people in the aporetic logic underlying the verity of climate change, which can by definition only be desperate.

The archiving of 'mother earth' in a framework of such liberal values more seriously validates its own particular cosmopolitan politics of transnational 'species citizenship' as universal by posing 'her' romantically as in opposition to the 'cruel treatment by human beings.' The usurpation of the radical difference of an entity that is quite obviously at odds with the idea of emancipation under the veneer of cosmopolitan solidarity represents that vital difference once more in such a way that it 'no longer makes a difference' to the hegemony of speed. After all, what happens is the dissemination of the Bolivian case and proposal throughout the global media as a major spectacle in slow motion.[18] Meanwhile, the Bolivian city dwellers are left to fend for themselves. This insurrection of 'mother earth' as a subject of rights therefore marks arguably the final death knell for anything and everything that does not succumb to the neo-liberal ideal. The final deficit of the critical democratic project becomes also obvious considering that the proposal is an attempt to give the failed United Nations climate debate in Copenhagen new life. The latter had failed to reach a workable consensus due to the vastly different positions of the close to 200 national actors in that debate.[19] Klein remarks for this reason in 'A New Climate Movement in Bolivia' that 'the real culprit of the [Copenhagen climate debate] breakdown *was democracy itself*' (emphasis mine). I suggest that this failure and renewal of the democratic process once more marks the oxymoronic *urgent need to slow down*; climate change as future risk needs a managerial solution now, but this urgent solution is mobilised time and again through the technologies and discourses of speed. Giving 'mother earth rights' as a way of further extending global citizenship is for that reason not at all 'refreshingly new' (1) as Bonni Rambatan, in an interesting extension of radical Italian thought, for instance, proposes in 'Are Trees the New Proletariat?' but is exceedingly worrisome. This is because the rhetoric of trees and such as new margins exhibits a nostalgic desire to become nature while inserting them—quite absurdly, one may add—into the grand scheme of liberation that has caused pollution in the first place. Seeing 'the earth' as a subject of rights hence amounts to an aggravated *madness* of humanism I showed was already present as a seed in 80s and 90s environmentalist texts. It does not only mark an attempt to subjugate and reduce 'her' once more to a set of calculable forces that is doomed to fail, but also reads as a desperate attempt to plead for a way out of the violent intensification of humanism. Who or what, one may also add, is this plea finally addressed to?

THE ECOLOGICAL LIMITS OF QUESTIONABILITY

This chapter has followed the aporetic logic intrinsic to new media and no-border activism all the way through to its current culmination into climate change activism. Climate change activism represents the truly globalised arrangement of Eucken's original *Aktivismus*, emerging from the ways in which the stakes for alter-globalist activism have been raised considerably due to the strategy of resistance having reached a cultural and socio-economic tipping point: the ideas and practices of emancipation and freedom no longer give rise to subversion. Instead, as I showed in the previous chapters, they have started to become complicit in speed, which in turn has accelerated widespread ecological damage. That climate change activism emerges out of the Eurocentrism that reflected the dominant version of humanism can be gathered from the fact that its mode of encapsulation of otherness—various peoples and eventually nature itself—was already indicated in the colonialist enterprise that precedes it. As such, speed-elitism is sexist, racist, hubristic, and unscrupulously non-sustainable even if it no longer operates simply in the service of 'the West' or 'the masculine.' In its place, I would even go as far as to say that signifiers like West and East, male and female, like action and thought, and margin and centre, have themselves become implicated in the incessant requirement for circulation and transaction of neo-liberal globalisation. This also explains why earlier concerns in more identity-based activism with gender, class, and race have been largely subsumed by and displaced into new media, no-border, and climate change activism. After reaching its tipping point, then, the liberatory rhetoric that grounds the reproduction of the speed-elite starts to (threaten to) fall in on itself as its aporias more and more engender a desperate attempt at simulating scientific and moral mastery and salvation to keep the dream of liberation alive. Climate change activism exemplifies that collapse by virtue of showing the limits of humanism as being the real ecological limits of capitalist expansion, progress, and innovation.

The system of communication and economic transaction that underlies the dissemination of awareness-raising movies, websites, and books always already presupposes the Promethean promise and premise that technological disaster and salvation reside in some just-out-of-reach future. It is this promise that today fuels—pun intended—environmental activism and philosophy, as well as its current disenfranchisement, negative fallout, and a near blissful yet anxious technological acceleration for the speed-elite. Speed-elitist politics nonetheless are increasingly based on the exaltation of whatever crosses national and disciplinary boundaries, in which the activist or political actor shares a technological perpetuation and globalisation of a certain questionable faith. This faith, combined with the curious logic of mediation, generates a widespread acceptance of a very particular version of the 'truth' that seems to have as its prime outcome to reflect back to us who we believe we are and what we believe we can do. But it is also the *questionability* of this humanist faith that allows it to be transformed and propelled forward in the name of justice in the first place. We see here perhaps not merely a double, but a manifold affirmation taking place; but as much as this affirmation happens within the non-neutral space of the technical-economical calculation of risk, it tends to dissimulate its deconstruction. Eventually, though, there is an aporia at work in all these well-meant mobilisations, in which the unintended effects of these mobilisations themselves oddly spiral into calls for even more vigorous technological, academic, and political activity. It is hence by virtue of apocalyptic thought that alter-globalism may again regain its promissory status, but not without sadly initially doing a whole lot of damage.

5 Accelerating Deceleration
Out of the Cinders of Activism

This strategy of interpretation is also a politics. The extreme ambiguity of the gesture consists in saving a body of thought by damning it.

Jacques Derrida, *Of Spirit: Heidegger and the Question* (73).

The only justification for thinking and writing is that it accelerates these terminal processes. Here, beyond the discourse of truth, resides the poetic and enigmatic value of thinking.

Jean Baudrillard, *The Vital Illusion* (83).

I have reached the provisional end of my trajectory through some exemplary and remarkable forms of contemporary alter-globalist activism. Starting with the energetic enthusiasm of new media activism, following through with the indignation of no-border activism, and finally arriving at the bafflements of climate change activism, the limits of what these activisms as well as my deconstructive query have to offer have for now been reached. This journey through these activist ideas represents in many ways also a personal journey, always guided by the spirit of justice that ultimately underpins all these pursuits. As much as this spirit has today gone 'viral,' its limitations have shown themselves in how the alter-globalist work of justice, done through these intellectual and activist endeavours, is more and more inextricably wound up in the neo-liberal quest for speed. This quest for speed, which is in many ways an outgrowth of European humanism and its faith in technological progress, finds its partial materialisation in current new information, archiving, transportation, and communication technologies and their promise of emancipation, control, and transcendence. This speed-elitism facilitates the neo-liberal conditions of possibility that seek to dissimulate, again through these technologies of mediation, the resource- and labour-intensive exacerbation of inequalities that its emancipatory fantasy thrives on. Many well-meaning alter-globalist thinkers, like Hardt and Negri, Harris, or Lovink and Bey, indeed explicitly or implicitly centre much of their politics on the discourses and imaginations of border-crossing, freedom, connection, mobility, and the subject-agent reminiscent of Eurocentrism that today surround these new technologies. My analysis of complicities should be a warning for academic studies that romanticise alter-globalist activisms as the next 'revolutionary' movement or project that will save the world from the ills of neo-liberalism. The unremitting loyalty and praise of certain researchers vis-à-vis alter-globalist activists, especially within new social-movement studies, surely pays heed to the promise of emancipation. But it also runs the risk of irresponsibly repeating those discourses of speed and their material underpinnings that sadly exacerbate current inequalities. Too much undiscerning loyalty thus betrays the activist spirit in an irresponsible way, because it fails to tease out the complicities of activism in *Aktivismus* and acceleration. Uncomplicated celebrations of alter-globalisation are therefore paradoxically rather *dis*loyal to the idealism and promise of justice that informs these activisms.

So we need the complications of deconstruction to keep the activist spirit alive, and ever more carefully so. Because lest the reader is under the illusion that with the recent revolt in the Arab world and anti-corporate 'Occupy' activism in the West things are looking better, the trend of the growing complicity of activism in acceleration is in fact continuously worsening. The celebrations of how social media supposedly aided 'the' Arab Spring reproduce even starker the post-colonial and hyper-modern conditions through which speed-elitism operates. The representation of the moral positivity of the Arab citizens' supposed 'cry for democracy' is a point in case. This is not to say that the outrage of the Arab citizens is not valid, but that it is just as much part of that 'coercive situation disguised as an invitation' of global neo-liberalism. In keep with the complicity of the humanist endeavour with speed namely, the Arab world has to be 'democratically' *annexed* and the failure of and disenchantment with democracy in the West has to be *negated* or suppressed. This is why numerous academic articles and newspapers in the case of the Arab Spring obsessively praise social media as 'the' tool for democratic change.[1] The Arab Spring hence showcases ever closely the ways in which the democratic promise is increasingly and desperately hallucinated into the latest media tools. What is more, the supposed victory of democracy in the Arab world circulates in the media by means of the typical romanticisation of the 'Eastern other.' We can see here again that technological acceleration runs through the formalisation of the two tropes characteristic of humanism, namely the fantasy of the subject-agent as the proper centre for revolution and action, as well as its reproduction of an ideal other. As I discussed in Chapter 3, this reproduction relies on the fantasy that these subjects' demands are *not* a product of global speed-elitism. In the global media, this runs through an incessant portrayal of 'the' Arab population supposedly authentically desiring 'freedom and democracy.' The fact that the protests are foremost a result of mass unemployment among young men is hence suppressed. It also obscures the various forms of strife and marginalisation internal to the Arab world, and dissimulates how speed-elitism had a strong hand in local and global unemployment and marginalisation. Social media then function perhaps for young Arab men as prostheses to compensate for the damage caused by speed-elitism.[2] Either way, the pornographic over-representation

in the media of Arab citizens protesting in the streets rings one of the many
death knells for global democracy, as what is really circulated and consumed in the media is an *image* of the public and of democracy, not its
exercise. The fact that the Arab protesters are parading signs with English
words like 'freedom,' 'Twitter,' and 'Facebook' on them is not so much
because these are desired or liberatory, but because the protests' spectacular imagery is set up for *consumption* by a global audience in dire need of
a re-affirmation of the humanist promise. In a similar vein, the sympathetic
Occupy Wall Street protests are consumed as images of resistance to quell
the sense of desperation in its global audience, while the occupation of
actual space itself has become a largely futile and outdated strategy under
speed-elitism. This is because real power has migrated into the accelerated
nodes of capital flows on which whims bankers themselves are just as much
dependent. One could almost say that the global speed-elitist media solicit
the protests in an effort to justify *themselves*, thereby implicating these
novel forms of activism once more in an exceedingly dodgy game.

What follows from all these complications of these activist and intellectual pursuits is that the politics of emancipation and of oppression con-
verge in their technologically enhanced fantasy to transcend contaminated
legacies and foster positive social change. As I hope to have shown in the
previous chapters, such politics makes the indulgence in this fantasy of
emancipation partly an actual possibility. But it seems that it so far does so
only for a select elite and various 'upwardly mobile' groups and individuals. While the emergence of the speed-elite reproduces certain gendered and
raced oppressions, a partial erasure of such markers simultaneously takes
place within the speed-elite itself because of the belief that its utopian vision
adheres to anyone who counts as 'human.' This implies a consolidation of
an exclusionary anthropocentrism—the problem of the new technologies
thus reflects itself back to us once more as the problem of 'the human' as
subject that so many post-structuralists have lifted out as the key issue when
thinking for and through justice. For activisms assuming the unequivocal
virtue of the politicised subject-agent, the stakes have hence been raised
considerably, and deconstruction is the prime way in which such stakes can
be adequately addressed. This is because it shows that, despite the fact that
alter-globalist activism tries to effectively counter current disenfranchisement under neo-liberalism, these activisms also intensify and accelerate
politics under neo-liberal globalisation—in other words, that the saintly
spirit of activism (and its subject) is today more than ever haunted by a
sort of evil twin. Every time we think we have pinned down the location
of that demon, it reappears with a vengeance *within* our very own devout
gesture of pinning down. We have ourselves in fact become the targets of
our objects of acceleration, at the same time as the objects of acceleration
give us our target or goal. This means that to conceive of the traditional
categories of left-wing and right-wing politics as each other's politically
oppositional adversaries, like many strands of the anti-European Union,

anti-banking, and anti-WTO activism do, is a misconception that dissimulates their *mutually* implicated nature in the emergence of the speed-elite and the generation of ever more disenfranchised peoples. This aggravation of inequalities occurs hence not despite but *because* of their well-intended activist ideas and endeavours. *And yet*, if we want to be responsible in the face of such misery today, we have to set all these complicit activities and concepts to work. The conundrum of our responsibility resides hence exactly in the fact that alter-globalist activism on the one hand propagates new technologies and discourses of speed, while on the other must condemn the oppressive powers that these technologies and discourses are part of. This is the reason why alter-globalist struggles seem to get ever more desperate—a desperation born out of a growing perplexity of how its good intentions end up as speed-elitist complicity. We saw the culmination of this bizarre logic already emerging in Indymedia's internal politics, and foregrounding itself most strongly in the panic around global warming and the urgency of climate change activism. The 'evil twin' here makes its ghostly appearance in the apocalyptic climate change model. This means that the devoutly accelerated attempt at the global erasure of borders reflects back to us its own iniquity—an instant of what, for example, Baudrillard in *Seduction* calls 'reversibility.'[3]

It then appears that, as the world finds itself in this maelstrom of acceleration, the only response would be to *urgently slow down* the mad aggravation of this tension and this unsustainable targeting logic. But what does this really mean or entail? It can certainly not mean a total abandonment of technological means to chase the promise of justice—if this were at all possible—even if deliverance from speed must partly lie beyond the idea of the subject as agent of her or his *technè*. After all, this book itself participates in the activist endeavour by means of accelerating the production and consumption of ideas through the double affirmation that is activism's deconstruction. Responsibility can only ever respond to its tainted legacy. And insofar as this book attempts to rekindle the activist flame, it must pay heed to the fact that this flame today is also provided with oxygen or air by technological means. So there is no redemption to be found here, in these pages or arguments. But what is more important is that all my analyses hint at a structural collapse of neo-liberal capitalism in the not-so-far future. This is because, if the internal contradiction that haunts activism is the primary asset of speed-elitism, then the mechanical intensification of this tension renders neo-liberal capitalism increasingly unstable, explosive, and unsustainable—a volatility that its successive crises also show. In other words, if alter-globalist activism is not total justice, then total speed-elitism is not possible either. And if activism accelerates the coming of speed-elitism's collapse, then this would simply be as welcome as much as it will be devastating. So although the conclusion of the immanent fatality of these complicities in speed appears as a most logical consequence of my argument, this conclusion nonetheless intriguingly displays an aporetic gap between the desperate pessimism it exhibits and the unshakable optimism and hope it professes. For in spite of my strong allegiance to and love for alter-globalist activism, I had to critique the complicities of these activisms in speed-elitism *in the name of* their very own spirit. One could say I had to do this because this spirit suffers today from an increasing 'inflammation' as Derrida calls it in *Of Spirit* (32), but of course any spirit is always already 'enflamed' or else it would not properly move activist and intellectual people like me. This then also means that the deconstruction of activism, as well as the argument to 'urgently slow down' *qua apocalyptic argument*, is just as much an illusory horizon of salvation on the landscape of speed-politics. Because of the productive restaging of the dialectic between action and thought I invoke here in the name of alter-globalist justice, the appeal to justice therefore pushes us into the abyss of speed as well as opening speed up to make way for its critique, and finally, *perhaps*, for its disappearance.

Deconstruction is therefore very much political, but not in the sense of providing a recipe or solution for activism. Is it political because it shows how it itself can only make an argument for deceleration by implicating itself in acceleration. In this way, it lays bare the vulnerability of speed-elitism's mechanics; the 'Achilles' heel' that illegitimate power always has. And therein lies precisely its promise. If this sounds like a useless programme, this is only because of the misplaced demand made on thinking today that it be 'practical'—because of, as Derrida says in *Of Spirit,* the mistaken expectation that 'philosophy ought at the very least to procure . . . a sort of compass for universal orientation' (42). But as I have shown throughout, such a demand for practicality is a demand thoroughly tainted by a mechanistic and instrumentalist ideology reminiscent of Eucken's economistic solution. If thought wants to remain critical of the injustices done in the name of such solutions, it *must defer* rash and self-righteous action. And it must do so, in light of the disasters of speed-elitism, *at great speed.*[4] Throughout my critical discussions of activism, then, one can see the contours of the formal logic of the operation of justice emerging of which the paradoxical injunction of 'urgently slowing down' is foremost (and perhaps only) a metaphor. Affirming the spirit of activism leads, quite simply, to the practical solution *as* a way of thinking. It points towards a thoughtful attitude and towards a recognition of the inevitable internal tension that this attitude requires. It demands that we remain attentive to this tension, especially when we as alter-globalists seem to know with such certainty what 'needs to be done.' Indymedia's politics, migrant activism, and environmentalist calls for cosmopolitanism indeed all display this *for justice indispensable tension*. So alter-globalist activism is just as much the one exemplary location where the promise of justice is to be re-found after its deconstructive detour.

So forced by the situation of acceleration into a questionable leap of faith, my final prediction will be this: sooner or later, alter-globalist activism—as much as the entire machinery of acceleration—will implode *due to* itself, with or without my help. Eventually, then, a glorious future free from oppression awaits the world *thanks to and despite of* alter-globalist activism and thought, which through all the muffled voices of despair in this new future will transcend into its beautiful completion.[5] This destination of alter-globalisms is its final and true deconstruction. This means that there is hope, as the future of neo-liberalism remains utterly undecided. Key to such hope is the insight that, while speed-elitism inevitably leads to major accidents due to the intensification (and not foreclosure) of politics, such an accident itself may also to everyone's surprise *announce the arrival of radical otherness.*

As always, the pronouncement of the demise of a body of thought will give it new life. It is a narrative of desperation and hope; a narrative of death and resurrection, and of hubris and self-flagellation. Now does not that tainted story sound familiar? We have come full circle again; but this time, I hope, with a difference.

Notes

NOTES TO CHAPTER 1

1. I should make clear here that the term 'alter-globalist' is by no means my own invention, but has circulated for many years among the groups and individuals in Europe who identify with the anti-globalisation movement, but who are not against globalisation *tout court*. I give the term a more self-reflexive spin by claiming that denouncing globalisation is not at all what most of these groups do—they are in fact an intricate part of globalisation's production and expansion.
2. I also argue from my own experience in many forms of contemporary activism that the events of May '68, while certainly being the 'last gasp' of a kind of classical protest that combined action with theory, does not figure at all anymore in the young alter-globalist activist imagination.
3. See Gerold Blümle and Nils Goldschmidt: 'Walter Eucken: Vordenker einer freiheitlichen Ordnung' ('Walter Eucken: Theorist of a Liberal Order').
4. One can of course also draw connections to the free-market politics of Thatcherism and Reaganomics, which both conceptualize 'freedom' in terms of deregulation. Neo-liberalism is therefore paradoxically linked to the democratic format of a 'market of opinions.' This renders its 'freedom' contradictory: to ensure that neo-liberalism functions, a democratic system must be *enforced* and disseminated.
5. 'Person, die im sozialistischen Wettbewerb durch wesentliche Erhöhung der Leistungen und durch neue Arbeitsmethoden die Produktion steigert.' 'Bewegung, die sich die höchstmögliche Produktionssteigerung in einem Betrieb zum Ziel gesetzt hat.' See *Duden Deutsches Universalwörterbuch*, edition 1989.
6. This point has also been repeatedly made by Jean Baudrillard, starting from his incisive 'For a Critique of the Political Economy of the Sign.'
7. The June 18, 1999, protest in London against the WTO started off peacefully, but later turned violent and became riotous. Some protesters blamed the London police for provoking the riots, but others blamed the more aggressive strands within the protest movement—in particular what later came to be known as the anarchist black bloc—for indulging in violence. Some anarchists argued that violence against people and goods of capitalist institutions was justified and only minimal compared to the global violence capitalism exhorts. They also claimed that violence was the only way for the protest to become spectacular and reach the news headlines. Other protesters argued in turn that such violence in the news would merely give the anti-globalisation movement a bad name, and that those anarchists were 'playing macho-cool.'

8. Derrida suggests indeed, in *Monolingualism of the Other or the Prosthesis of Origin*, that it is regularly under the usually well-intended banner of 'openness to the other' (40) or 'under alibis of universal humanism' (39) that the current spread of capitalist hegemony establishes itself.

9. In *Dissemination*, Derrida says, 'The fold multiplies itself but is not one' (50).

10. Nick Couldry and James Curran's *Contesting Media Power* is a good example of this. While they argue correctly in 'The Paradox of Media Power' that the media have an 'increasingly central dimension of power in contemporary societies,' they nonetheless reduce anti-globalization activism to 'contests over access' (4).

11. Not only Virilio but also writers like Bernard Stiegler have claimed that there is a fundamental relationship of technologies to speed. David Wills notes, for instance, in 'Techneology or the Discourse of Speed' that for Stiegler, 'the horizon of technology is speed because its origin is time' (239). This is so because our relation to time is always technologically informed.

12. I am indebted here to John Armitage's idea of the 'global kinetic elite' in 'Resisting the Neoliberal Discourse of Technology: The Politics of Cyberculture in the Age of the Virtual Class.'

13. Armitage and Roberts aptly call these disenfranchised groups in 'Chronotopia' the 'slower classes.' I will use this term a few times later on in this book.

14. Armitage and Roberts likewise conclude that 'The only problem is that the hallmark of this new social imaginary is . . . support for an inclusiveness that is utterly consonant with the continuation of existing political inequalities and exclusionary policies' (48).

15. This connection of new technologies with the notion of repetition and difference brings us full circle to the particularities of communication as elaborated by Derrida. In 'Signature Event Context,' Derrida contests the commonsense idea that communication through writing or tele-technologies appears simply as the extension of an authentic expression. Such an idea of straightforward extension presupposes that the space of communication is always homogenous, as well as that of the identity (of meaning). Instead, for any meaning to be transferable, meaning must always be able to 'have meaning' in the absence of the one writing or speaking it. This implies that the subject is 'never one with itself': the constitutive fantasy that the subject can completely intend or control meaning appears as an idealisation, anything short of which there is nothing but appears and 'a general displacement' (314). Therefore, the (technological) extension already changes the space of communication: intention gets displaced ever more forcefully through any tool (of communication) that the subject represents to itself as 'neutral' medium.

16. Such a dangerous hyper-modernism as the dominant function of post-modernism and its allegiance to the new technologies has been described by Albert Borgmann in 'Hyperreality' as 'Postmodernism shar[ing] with modernism an unreserved allegiance to technology, but differ[ing] from modernism in giving technology a hypercomplex design' (82).

17. The term 'enforceability' is from Derrida. In 'The Force of Law: The "Mystical Foundation of Authority," ' Derrida analyses the intricate relationship of justice, technologies, and force. Legitimating justice, by deciding and acting upon what is lawful or unlawful, righteous or evil, always implies force or at least *enforceability*. Therefore, a particular type of discursive (humanist) force, which paradoxically revolves around the rhetoric and acts of justice, may enhance itself considerably through those new technologies that are indeed designed for mastery and control through speed-elitism. This

continuous enhancement of a particular force agrees with the idea that the excessive logic of speed results in an intensifying repetition.

18. Many texts, from Zillah Eistenstein's *Global Obscenities* to Lisa Nakamura's 'Interrogating the Digital Divide,' have already pointed out that this violence and these exclusions sadly continue to work along lines of gender, class, and race, in particular through the feminisation and 'third-worldisation' of poverty, which paradoxically accompanies the economic rise of formerly 'underdeveloped' nations like India and China.

19. The term 'fatal strategy' is from Jean Baudrillard, who says, in *The Ecstasy of Communication,* 'If the world is fatal, let us be more fatal than it' (101). Arguably, Baudrillard may not say this in order to spur us on, but to hold a mirror to us in order to elucidate the absurdity of what we are doing.

20. I am referring here of course to Martha Nussbaum's condemnation of Judith Butler's post-structuralist work in 'The Professor of Parody.'

21. Tellingly, the *Oxford Dictionary and Thesaurus* also mentions that synonyms for 'impractical' are 'academic' and 'theoretical' (Oxford University Press, 2001).

22. For instance, the largest record label for white power music in the United States is *Resistance Records*, and many Aryan groups regard 'virile' action and violence as essential for the struggle against 'other races.'

23. The works of Edmund Husserl, Martin Heidegger, and Maurice Merleau-Ponty spring to mind here, as well as that of many feminist scholars of science.

24. For this reason, Gayatri Spivak remarks, in 'Criticism, Feminism, and the Institution,' that 'the privileging of practice is in fact no less dangerous than the vanguardism of theory' (2).

25. Evidence that the boundaries between activism and intellectualism are fluid and complex, with activists and academics producing theories as well as being involved in political practices, shows when academics such as Noam Chomsky, Henry Giroux, Judith Butler, or the late Edward Said do political activism by means of their theories.

26. In 'Criticism, Feminism, and The Institution,' Spivak puts it nicely when discussing the relationship between 'textuality/deconstruction and the field of politics.' Against theorists or activists who regard practice as pure action and theory as mere thought (or practice as mere action and theory as pure thought), Spivak correctly cautions that 'Practice is an irreducible *theoretical* moment, no practice takes place without presupposing itself as an example of some more or less powerful theory . . . the intellectual or anti-intellectual who can choose to privilege practice and then create a practice/theory split within a sort of theory, in fact, is also capable, because he or she is [just as much] produced by the institution' (2, italics mine).

27. The vocation of the left-wing intellectual and activist that Derrida speaks of resides in a morality that bases itself on the practical-political quest for 'greater individual freedom in culture and broader democracy in the economy and society,' as Cornel West calls it in 'Theory, Pragmatisms, and Politics' (36), and many of us activists will recognise this aim.

28. I thank my activist colleague Paul Treanor in 'Neoliberalism: Origins, Theory, Definition' for this astute phrasing.

29. This agrees with Audre Lorde's famous claim in *Sister Outsider* that 'the master's tools will never dismantle the master's house' (110).

30. Even though new-media activism can potentially incorporate those activist endeavours that critique (the use of) new media, I will use the term 'new-media activism' throughout this book to refer to those groups and individuals who—either implicitly or explicitly—argue that new and social media

technologies are liberatory or who 'religiously' use these technologies for activist purposes.

31. See, for instance, Jean Baudrillard's infamous *Seduction*, which harvested lots of criticism from feminist scholars for that reason. I claim nonetheless that Baudrillard makes a point about the subject under technocratic conditions of simulation that feminist theory very much should pick up on.

32. Derrida notes in 'The Ear of the Other' that one needs to be able to identify with something in a text in order to critique it, claiming that 'My relation to these texts is characterised by *loving jealousy* and not at all by nihilistic fury' (87, italics mine).

33. See also Peggy Kamuf's reading of deconstruction as a form of jealousy in 'Deconstruction and Love.'

34. The term 'movement of movements' appeared first in Italy and is commonly used to describe the alter-globalisation movement.

35. Examples here are numerous. I will mention here only in passing Barry K. Gills's *Globalization and the Politics of Resistance*, Mitzi Waltz's *Alternative and Activist Media*, and Van de Donk and Loader's *Cyberprotest*.

NOTES TO CHAPTER 2

Some parts of this chapter were previously published as 'Activism, Academia, and the Humanist Aporia' in *Cultural Politics*, Vol. 5, No.2. ©2009 Berg Publishers. All rights reserved.

1. A more detailed historical analysis of how new media activism partly came out of certain anarchist movements and ideas of the 1970s is unfortunately beyond the scope of this book. Conceptions about the supposed non-hierarchy of the Internet and particular strands of anti-authoritarianism share obviously some common ground.

2. Good examples of such criticisms are Peter van Aalst and Stefaan Walgrave's 'New Media, New Movements?' as well as W. Lance Bennett's 'New Media Power,' which argues aptly that 'the preeminent uses of global communications networks remain the efforts of corporations and governments to strengthen the neoliberal economic regime' (18).

3. John Armitage and Phil Graham in 'Dromoeconomics: Towards a Political Economy of Speed' likewise conclude that hyper-capitalism is the system within which forms of thought and language are formally subsumed under capital. (114)

4. An intriguing aspect of the B92 campaign that came to my ears during my work for HelpB92 in Amsterdam (which was indirectly funded by the Dutch government) was that its related youth movement OTPOR! (Resistance!) received generous funding for their campaigns from certain Western corporations. OTPOR! also received an MTV Europe 'Free Your Mind' Award later that year. B92 is now a respectable commercial radio and TV station in Serbia.

5. Terry Eagleton discusses this co-existence briefly in his amusing 'The Enlightenment Is Dead! Long Live the Enlightenment!'

6. One could think here, for instance, of the many feminist analyses that draw out the masculinist and white bias in the medical sciences, or that relate contemporary militaristic compulsions to capitalist expansion, masculinity, and Eurocentrism.

7. This argument is inspired by one typically vilified 'post-modern' intellectual: Jean Baudrillard, and in particular his 'The Implosion of Meaning in the Media.'

8. W. Lance Bennett remarks similarly in 'New Media Power' that under conditions of post-industrial fragmentation 'people are more likely to discover

the self as an active project,' which he in turn connects to the emergence of Internet activism (28). Bennett nonetheless holds that such activism, due to the distributed nature of networks, 'becomes potentially transformative' (20). This is precisely the *promise* of positive social change that I argue is intimately related to humanism and its tools and assumptions.

9. Baudrillard aptly states in 'The Implosion' that 'All the movements that only play on liberation, emancipation, on the resurrection of a subject of history ... do not see that they are going in the direction of the system, whose imperative today is precisely the overproduction and regeneration of meaning and speech' (86).

10. It is telling that Baudrillard himself engages in the exact same (media) strategies of the subject by publishing such an engaging and argumentative political article. This leaves one to arrive at a number of conclusions: that perhaps he is somehow attempting to stage the logic of the system ('The Implosion' as performative interpretation), that he actually still has faith in the difference that the hyper-real repetition of communicating thought might make, or that he wants to drive the system to its logical extreme, which would be the 'catastrophe ... of productive finality' (83). Or, he does all of the above. I will return to the implications of these ambiguities in the final chapter.

11. The amount of research done on the Indymedia project, usually within new social-movement studies, has skyrocketed so much in the first years of the 21st century that Indymedia editors, myself included, started complaining on several lists about the incessant requests for information and interviews.

12. Parasite comes from the Greek *para* (by, besides) and *sitos* (food) and means literally 'by-eater.'

13. Media-activist Paul Garrin suggested at the Next5Mintes3 conference that term 'permanent autonomous network,' inspired by Hakim Bey, be adopted for Indymedia style activism. See Pit Schultz's interview with Garrin.

14. Hudson refers here in particular to the escalating Israel-Palestine conflict in 2002, and claims that the Kosovo war would not have happened if Indymedia would have had a strong presence in that region.

15. Nick Couldry also notices this structural tension between the vision of equality and the push for openness in the Indymedia project in 'Beyond the Hall of Mirrors?' He asks whether Indymedia consumers 'are postmodern readers who happily accept that all truth is relative? Or are they committed to the rightness of a certain view of the world and its inequities?' (47)

16. A good example of this I watched from nearby were the extremely racist and sexist remarks that followed a timely posting by Nadia Fadil about the stereotyping of Muslim women in Belgian politics on IMC-Belgium in 2003.

17. Literally 'we are not we.' The original slogan from subcomandante Marcos was 'we are you,' indicating that, like the Zapatistas, everybody is today wound up in neo-liberal capitalism. This slogan has lead many activists to equate their own desires and struggles with those of the Zapatistas, creating in turn huge visibility for Zapatismo. One could, however, wonder what this heroisation of Zapatismo has in the end really done for the peasants in Chiapas themselves, besides their becoming the poster children for alterglobalism, and Marcos becoming its romantic hero.

18. Cleaver has written various pieces on the supposed revolutionary force of activist uses of new technologies and their nascence in the Zapatista movement. His articles 'Computer-Linked Social Movements and the Global Threat to Capitalism' and 'The Zapatistas and the Electronic Fabric of Struggle' have informed many new-media activist analyses. I will not go into his work here, because he has not written explicitly about Indymedia.

19. C3I is a Cold War acronym and refers to 'communications, command, control and intelligence.' The term is shorthand for the infrastructure and geopolitical strategy required for distant and near-instantaneous military action and control by a centralised command headquarters.
20. I take it that it is for this reason that Paul Virilio exclaims in *Pure War* that 'the delirium surrounding the Net is a paroxysmal form of propaganda' (199–200).

NOTES TO CHAPTER 3

A rough and abridged version of this chapter was earlier published as 'The Migrant Metaphor in Radical Italian Thought' in *Cultural Studies Review*, Vol. 11, No. 2 (2005).
1. All these organisations were quick to have their own websites: see http://www.contrast.org/borders/kein/archiv.html and http://www.antimedia.net/nooneisillegal/, http://www.xs4all.nl/~ac/, http://www.no-border.org/news_index.php.
2. See http://www.antimedia.net/xborder/, http://www.baxterwatch.net/ and http://woomera2002.antimedia.net/. Also, there is typically a lot of cross-posting on Indymedia websites of the issues debated on these no-border websites.
3. This can be deduced from a quick search in the manifold of library resources and online databases, for instance, Questia at http://www.questia.com/Index.jsp.
4. 'Single issue style campaigning' consists, according to Foster, of 'an issue, a network of well resourced, influential activist groups, some slightly tokenistic links to especially oppressed people, a well designed electronic interface and plenty of publicity in the anti-capitalist media' (1–2).
5. The term 'autonomia' is actually a contested term and points by no means to a homogeneous group. For a good discussion of the constitution of 'autonomia' and the power struggles within and on the borders of 'autonomia,' see Patrick Cunninghame's interview with Sergio Bologna.
6. See also Michael Ryan: 'The Theory of Autonomy' and Brett Neilson: 'Italy in Translation.'
7. On the role of migrant factory workers within *autonomia,* see George Katsiaficas's 'Italian Autonomia' (19, 1997).
8. 'The Libre Culture Manifesto' by David Berry and Giles Moss, which problematically likens the 'caged creativity' of the Italian 60s factory workers to the 'subversive' creativity of software programmers, is a good example of this.
9. Spivak therefore notes infamously in 'Marginality in the Teaching Machine': 'The well-placed . . . [activist or] academic can *afford* to find [a situation] deplorable' (54, italics mine). Such actors become for Spivak proponents of Eurocentrism, since they are a 'group susceptible to upward mobility' that thrive on posing as 'authentic inhabitants of the [non-Western] margin' (59). I argue here that Eurocentrism has given way to a more vicious 'speed-centrism.'
10. Derrida illustrates the dangers of the pretences of equality in alliance, which falsely imagines a common goal and a shared history of fighting against oppression amongst allied groups, well in a brief paragraph in *Monolingualism of the Other* on the hyphen between 'Franco-Maghrebian.' 'The silence of that hyphen,' says Derrida, 'does not appease anything, not a single torment' (11).

11. In *A Critique of Postcolonial Reason*, Spivak concludes that '[the] broad politics [of global development] is the subaltern as the rhetoric of their protest' and calls this role of a metaphorical subaltern in service of Western hegemony the 'native informant' (373).
12. Spivak likewise remarks that 'liberation theologies are narratives of individual transcendence in sacrifice' (97).
13. A border-hacker is someone who sets up camp near a heavily trafficked national border and uses new communication technologies to connect across national borders in order to act out their freedom of 'reverse engineering' (in the fashion of Lovink and Schneider). Border-hack events usually take the form of a new-media arts festival, much like the Next Five Minutes festivals, although the main focus is on migration.
14. See also Arianna Bove and Erik Empson's succinct analysis in 'The Dark Side of the Multitude.'
15. A good example of this would be Paolo Virno's 'Virtuosity and Revolution: The Political Theory of Exodus.'
16. Bove and Empson do admit that 'in this framework ... some powerful struggles of re-appropriation do take place.' See 'The Dark Side of the Multitude' (1).
17. For an excellent discussion on how the concept of 'empire' falls short in the Canadian political and activist context around border disputes and narratives of 'frontiers,' see Ian Angus's 'Empire, Borders, Place: A Critique of Hardt and Negri's Concept of Empire.'
18. For Haraway's own much more ambiguous conception of the cyborg and its relation to military and imperialist violence, see 'A Cyborg Manifesto: Science, Technology and Socialist-Feminism in the Late Twentieth Century.'
19. Timothy Brennan in 'The Italian Ideology' tellingly calls *Empire* 'so cheery and, if one can put it this way, so *American*' despite Hardt and Negri's 'erudite renditions of European theories' (99).
20. All these terms are implicit references to computer jargon: 'makeworlds' is a UNIX command, and 'border=0' is hypertext markup language. I would like to point out that 'border=0, location=yes' is a total contradiction in terms when one conceives of embodiment as necessarily situated.
21. See http://www.fibreculture.org.
22. This information was passed to me by an acquaintance who was present at this particular no-border action.
23. Indymedia Sydney conceived of this temporary Indymedia camp near Woomera, also questionably referred to with the US-Iraq war code 'Desert Storm,' as having the same function as the border-hack festivals. See also http://antimedia.net/desertstorm/. The use of 'Desert Storm' tellingly points to the intricate relationship between new-media activism and military hegemony.
24. The reference to the Zapatistas is in this case particularly misguided, because subcomandante Marcos has regularly proclaimed that he wants to defend the construction of Mexico as a nation-state *with* definite borders. See, for instance, http://mondediplo.com/1997/09/marcos.
25. See, for instance, http://library.sievxmemorial.org/agoddard001.htm, http://amsterdam.nettime.org/Lists-Archives/nettime-bold-0204/msg00106.html, http://archives.econ.utah.edu/archives/aut-op-sy/2002m04/msg00016.htm, and many more.
26. I thank Ryan Bishop and John Phillips for the term 'hallucination of radical alterity.' See, for instance, their 'Diasporic Communities and Identity Politics.'

NOTES TO CHAPTER 4

1. See especially Paul Virilio's *The Original Accident* and his interview with Louise Wilson called 'The Museums of Accidents.'
2. Good examples of this are, for instance, Christopher Norris's *Uncritical Theory* and Douglas Kellner's *Jean Baudrillard: From Marxism to Postmodernism and Beyond*, despite the latter's sympathetic attitude to Baudrillard's work. Rather than claiming that reality does not exist or that simulation is 'inaccurate' representation, I would claim that Baudrillard draws out the compulsion to oppose representation and reality in metaphysical thinking ever since Plato, which also returns in activism and intellectual work that must point out 'the real' behind the veil of ideology (as this book also does).
3. This is also the meaning of Derrida's 'there is no outside-text' in *Of Grammatology* (158); not that there is no real, but that there is no language that has unmediated access to the real.
4. A good example of such work, which is excellent in its field but nonetheless reproduces the artificial distinction between theory and object in its analysis of media representation as mere content provider, is Kris Wilson's 'Communicating Climate Change through the Media.'
5. Joost van Loon, referencing Martin Heidegger's work on technology, likewise aptly states in 'Mediating the Risks of Virtual Environments' that 'Risk society calls upon the very same technoscience to both reveal and conceal the danger' (236).
6. Paul Virilio, in fact, argues that this techno-logic first emerged out of the relationship between war and visual technologies, of which film is also part; see especially *War and Cinema: The Logistics of Perception* (84).
7. Jean Baudrillard artfully plays with this confusion over the subject-object distinction and the appearance of agency of objects, as some sort of return of the repressed that marks our era of acceleration in *The System of Objects* (142).
8. Of course, I also exhibit a form of self-flagellation when pointing out my own activist naivety in this book.
9. We can see that the Roman strategy of *divide et impera*, which the British also used for their colonial enterprise, is thoroughly at work in speed-elitism. John Maguire likewise recognizes in 'The Tears inside the Stone' in the generation of fear one of the fundamental strategies of disciplining individuals into competitive survival mode under neo-liberalism; the very real experience of such fear hence crystallizes in the apocalyptic climate-change prediction.
10. Derrida claims in *Archive Fever* that 'the technical structure of the *archiving* archive [or, the archive in the process of archiving] also determines the structure of the archivable content' (17). The archive consequently calls into existence, rather than simply records. Since 'archivable meaning is codetermined by the structure that archives' (18), an inextricable part of it is the belief in the emancipatory virtue of archiving. Such a belief, I suggest, mirrors the humanist notion of the autonomous agent as mastering its tools and communicating its intentions transparently. In effect, this humanist system of belief is folded into contemporary technology in order to make such technology productive under neo-liberalism—the moral call hence informs reproduction.
11. In *World at Risk*, Beck stresses that reflexive modernization indeed means that 'we are not living in a post-modern world but in a *hyper*-modern world.' This is because the state and the military, as risk-producing risk managers, are 'becoming part of the problem they are supposed to solve' (55).
12. The term 'irrational rationality' is used by Armitage and Graham in 'Dromo-economics' to describe the rise of a pervasive managerialism that is in their assessment 'sociopathic' (112).

13. Contra thinkers like Rosi Braidotti, then, who argue that a feminist life-affirming politics should be mounted to oppose the masculine necro-politics of late-capitalism in, for instance, 'Bio-Power and Necro-Politics,' I would argue that the affirmation of life is part and parcel of this culture of death, and that the philosophical distinction between managed life (bios) and intrinsic life (zoë) is part and parcel of its contemporary politics.

14. A 2007 Stanford University research report (available at http://sites.amd. com/us/Documents/svrpwrusecompletefinal.pdf) estimated that the Internet (peripherals not included) was responsible for 868 billion kWh per year or about 6% of the total world energy consumption, and rising.

15. It is now quite common knowledge that Al Gore's 'green' politics apparently justified the excessive use of media (Internet, television, film) and transportation technologies (air travel) to disseminate the green message globally.

16. Virilio's assessment of hyper-modern societies as 'cinematic societies' (27, 1999), which I discussed in Chapter 3, seems again surprisingly apt here.

17. See Jaymi Heimbuch's 'Arguing with a Climate Change Skeptic? There's an App for That' on a 'green' corporate website called Treehugger.

18. A good example of this is the BBC coverage plus dramatic video 'Glacier threat to Bolivia capital' on http://news.bbc.co.uk/2/hi/8394324.stm.

19. See 'Low targets, goals dropped: Copenhagen ends in failure' on http://www.guardian.co.uk/environment/2009/dec/18/copenhagen-deal.

NOTES TO CHAPTER 5

1. The amount of newspaper articles and academic papers that absurdly claim that social media brought democracy to the Arab world is truly astounding. One only needs to search online for 'Arab Spring' and 'social media' to get hundreds of academic and journalistic hits claiming exactly this.

2. The 'social' in the phrase 'social media' points of course towards the Baudrillardian 'implosion of the social.' It also illustrates Virilio's claim in *Speed and Politics* that we are witnessing a *disappearance* of the social into the media.

3. Baudrillard's notion of seduction into or by the reversible form is in fact akin to Derrida's notion of deconstruction. In *Seduction*, he writes that reversibility 'abolishes the differential opposition' (12). Also, seduction takes place by something or someone radically heterogeneous to the system, which corresponds to Derrida's notion of deconstruction as make space for the radically other.

4. Here, we find an instance of Baudrillard's 'reversibility' in the conclusion of this book itself, since at this stage the concept of speed-elitism has exhausted itself, just as speed-elitism as such will eventually give way to something else (and hopefully something better). In other words, the totality of speed-elitism, being an enabling concept or metaphor just like 'slowing down,' *objectively does not exist*, even if the speed-elite itself is a very real entity.

5. ' "Because" and "although" at the same time,' says Jacques Derrida therefore in *Of Spirit*, 'that's the logical form of the tension which makes all this thinking hum' (108).

Bibliography

Agamben, Giorgio. 'Beyond Human Rights.' *Radical Thought in Italy: A Potential Politics*. Ed. Paolo Virno and Michael Hardt. Minneapolis: University of Minnesota Press, 1996: 159–166.

Angus, Ian. *Primal Scenes of Communication. Communication, Consumerism, and Social Movements*. Albany: State University of New York Press, 2000.

Angus, Ian. 'Empire, Borders, Place: A Critique of Hardt and Negri's Concept of Empire.' *Theory and Event*, Vol. 7, No. 3 (2004).

Anti-Racist Group for Free Flooding, n.d. Web. October 2005. <http://www.anti-media.net/nooneisillegal/>.

Armitage, John. 'Resisting the Neoliberal Discourse of Technology: The Politics of Cyberculture in the Age of the Virtual Class.' *CTheory.net*, 3 January 1999. Web. 22 April 2003. <http://www.ctheory.net/printer.asp?id=111>.

Armitage, John. 'From Modernism to Hypermodernism and Beyond. An Interview with Paul Virilio.' *Theory, Culture and Society*, 16.5–6. London: Sage (1999): 25–55.

Armitage, John. 'Ontological Anarchy, the Temporary Autonomous Zone, and the Politics of Cyberculture.' *Angelaki. Machinic Modulations: New Cultural Theory and Technopolitics*, 4.2, September (1999).

Armitage, John, and Joanne Roberts. 'Chronotopia.' *Living with Cyberspace. Technology & Society in the 21st Century*. London: Continuum, 2002: 43–54.

Armitage, John, and Phil Graham. 'Dromoeconomics: Towards a Political Economy of Speed.' *Parallax*, Vol. 7, No. 1 (2001): 111–123.

Arnison, Matthew. 'Open Publishing Is the Same as Free Software.' *Cat@lyst*, 2001. Web. March 2004.<http://www.cat.org.au/maffew/cat/openpub.html>.

Autonoom Centrum, n.d. Web. March 2004. <http://www.xs4all.nl/~ac/>.

Barker, Colin, and Laurence Cox. ' "What Have the Romans Ever Done for Us?" Academic and Activist Forms of Movement Theorising.' 2003. Web. September 2004. <http://www.iol.ie/~mazzoldi/toolsforchange/afpp/afpp8.html>.

Baudrillard, Jean. 'For a Critique of the Political Economy of the Sign.' *Jean Baudrillard: Selected Writings*. Ed. Mark Poster. Stanford, CA: Stanford University Press, 2001: 60–100.

Baudrillard, Jean. *The Ecstasy of Communication*. New York: Autonomedia, 1988.

Baudrillard, Jean. *Seduction*. Transl. Brian Singer. Basingstoke, UK: Macmillan Press,1990.

Baudrillard, Jean. 'The Implosion of Meaning in the Media.' *Simulacra and Simulation*. Ann Arbor: University of Michigan Press, 1994: 79–86.

Baudrillard, Jean. *The Vital Illusion*. New York: Columbia University Press, 2000.

Baudrillard, Jean. *The System of Objects*. Transl. James Benedict. New York: Verso, 1996.

Baxterwatch, n.d. Web. October 2004. <http://www.baxterwatch.net/>.

Beck, Ulrich. *World at Risk*. Transl. Ciaran Cronin. Cambridge: Polity, 2009.

Beckerman, Gal. 'Emerging Alternatives. Edging Away from Anarchy.' *Columbia Journalism Review*. Issue 5, September 2003. New York: Columbia University Press. Web. June 2005. <http://www.cjr.org/issues/2003/5/>.

Bennett, Lance W. 'New Media Power. The Internet and Global Activism.' *Contesting Media Power: Alternative Media in a Networked World*. Ed. Nick Couldry and James Curran. Lanham, MD: Rowman & Littlefield, 2003: 17–38.

Berry, David, and Giles Moss. 'The Libre Culture Manifesto.' *Free Software Magazine*, Issue 2, March 2005. Web. August 2006. <http://www.freesoftwaremagazine.com/free_issues/issue_02/pdfs/FSM_issue_02_libre_manifesto.pdf>.

Bey, Hakim. *The Temporary Autonomous Zone. Ontological Anarchy, Poetic Terrorism*. New York: Autonomedia, 1991.

Bishop, Ryan, and John Phillips. 'Diasporic Communities and Identity Politics: Containing the Political.' *Asian Diasporas. Cultures, Identities, Representations*. Ed. Robbie Goh and Shawn Wong. Hong Kong: Hong Kong University Press, 2004: 159–173.

Blümle, Gerold, and Nils Goldschmidt. 'Walter Eucken—Vordenker einer freiheitlichen Ordnung.' *Wisu—Das Wirtschaftsstudium*, 32: 1027–1030 (2003).

Borgmann, Albert. 'Hyperreality.' *Crossing the Postmodern Divide*. Chicago: University of Chicago Press, 1992: 82–96.

Boud. 'Can Independent, Grassroots Iranian Media Stop US Attack on Iran?' *The IMC-Europe Archives*. 2 April 2005, Web. April 2010. <http://lists.indymedia.org/pipermail/imc-europe/2005-April/0402-yz.html>.

Bove, Arianna, and Erik Empson. 'The Dark Side of the Multitude.' *MakeWorlds-Neuro—Networking Europe*, 23 September 2003. Web. September 2004. <http://www.makeworlds.org/book/view/36>.

Braidotti, Rosi. 'Bio-Power and Necro-Politics.' 2007. Web. October 2010. <http://www.let.uu.nl/~rosi.braidotti/personal/files/biopower.pdf>.

Brennan, Timothy. 'The Italian Ideology.' *Debating Empire*. Ed. Gopal Balakrishnan. London: Verso, 2003: 97–120.

Butler, Judith. 'Competing Universalities.' *Contingency, Hegemony, Universality. Contemporary Dialogues on the Left*. Ed. Judith Butler, Ernesto Laclau, and Slavoj Žižek. London: Verso, 2000: 136–181.

Butler, Judith. 'Subjects of Sex/Gender/Desire.' *The Cultural Studies Reader*. Ed. Simon During. London: Routledge, 1999: 340–353.

Butler, Judith: 'Dynamic Conclusions.' *Contingency, Hegemony, Universality. Contemporary Dialogues on the Left*. Ed. Judith Butler, Ernesto Laclau, and Slavoj Žižek. London: Verso, 2000: 263–280.

Cleaver, Harry. 'The Zapatistas and the Electronic Fabric of Struggle.' November 1995. Web. April 2005. <http://www.eco.utexas.edu/facstaff/Cleaver/zaps.html>.

Cleaver, Harry. 'Computer-Linked Social Movements and the Global Threat to Capitalism.' July 1999. Web. June 2002. <http://www.eco.utexas.edu/faculty/Cleaver/polnet.html>.

'Consensus Decision Making.' *Los Angeles Independent Media Center Collective Docs*, n.d. Web. March 2004. <http://la.indymedia.org/LA_IMC_Docs_001.html>.

Couldry, Nick. 'Beyond the Hall of Mirrors? Some Theoretical Reflections on the Global Contestation of Media Power.' *Contesting Media Power: Alternative Media in a Networked World*. Ed. Nick Couldry and James Curran. Lanham, MD: Rowman & Littlefield, 2003: 39–56.

Couldry, Nick, and James Curran. 'The Paradox of Media Power.' *Contesting Media Power: Alternative Media in a Networked World*. Lanham, MD: Rowman & Littlefield, 2003: 3–16.

Cronon, William. 'The Trouble with Wilderness; or, Getting Back to the Wrong Nature.' *Uncommon Ground: Rethinking the Human Place in Nature*. New York: Norton and Co, 1995: 69–90.

Cunninghame, Patrick. 'For an Analysis of Autonomia—An Interview with Sergio Bologna.' *libcom.org library*, June 1995. Web. June 2006. <http://libcom.org/library/analysis-of-autonomia-interview-sergio-bologna-patrick-cunninghame>.

Dean, Jodi. 'Communicative Capitalism: Circulation and the Foreclosure of Politics.' *Cultural Politics* 1.1. Oxford: Berg Publishers, 2005: 51–73.

DeLuca, Kevin. 'A Wilderness Environmentalism Manifesto: Contesting the Infinite Self-Absorption of Humans.' *Environmental Justice and Environmentalism: The Social Justice Challenge to the Environmental Movement*. Ed. Ronald Sandler and Phaedra Pezzullo. Cambridge, MA: MIT Press, 2007: 27–56.

Derive Approdi. 'luoghi comuni: il movimento globale come spazio di politicizzazione.' Rome: Derive Approdi, 2003.

Derrida, Jacques. *Of Spirit: Heidegger and the Question*. Chicago: University of Chicago Press, 1989.

Derrida, Jacques. 'Of an Apocalyptic Tone Newly Adopted in Philosophy.' *Derrida and Negative Theology*. Ed. Harold Coward and Toby Foshay. Albany: State University of New York Press, 1992: 25–79.

Derrida, Jacques. 'Force of Law: The "Mystical Foundation of Authority." ' *Deconstruction and the Possibility of Justice*. Ed. Drucilla Cornell, Michel Rosenfeld, and David Gray Carlson. New York: Routledge, 1992: 3–67.

Derrida, Jacques. 'Politics and Friendship. A Discussion with Jacques Derrida.' Centre for Modern French Thought, University of Sussex. December 1997. Web. November 2004. <http://www.sussex.ac.uk/Units/frenchthought/derrida.htm>.

Derrida, Jacques. 'The Future of the Profession or the University without Condition (Thanks to the "Humanities", What Could Take Place Tomorrow).' *Jacques Derrida and the Humanities: A Critical Reader*. Ed. Tom Cohen. Cambridge: Cambridge University Press, 2002: 24–67.

Derrida, Jacques. 'The Laws of Reflection. Nelson Mandela: In Admiration.' *For Nelson Mandela*. Ed. Jacques Derrida and Mustapha Tlili. New York: Seaver Books, 1987: 11–42.

Derrida, Jacques. 'Wears and Tears (Tableau of an Ageless World).' *Specters of Marx: The State of the Debt, the Work of Mourning, and the New International*. New York: Routledge, 1994: 77–94.

Derrida, Jacques. *Archive Fever: A Freudian Impression*. Transl. Eric Prenowitz. Chicago: University of Chicago Press, 1996.

Derrida, Jacques. *Monolingualism of the Other or the Prosthesis of Origin*. Transl. Patrick Mensah. Stanford, CA: Stanford University Press, 1998.

Derrida, Jacques. *Of Grammatology*. Transl. Gayatri Chakravorty Spivak. Baltimore: Johns Hopkins University Press, 1976.

Derrida, Jacques. 'Mochlos, or: The Conflict of the Faculties.' *Logomachia: The Conflict of the Faculties*. Ed. Richard Brand. Lincoln: University of Nebraska Press, 1993: 1–34.

Derrida, Jacques. 'Provocation: Forewords.' *Without Alibi*. Ed. and transl. Peggy Kamuf. Stanford, CA: Stanford University Press, 2002: xv–xxxv.

Derrida, Jacques. *Dissemination*. Transl. and intro. Barbara Johnson. Chicago: University of Chicago Press, 1981.

Derrida, Jacques. *The Ear of the Other*. New York: Bison Books, 1988.

Derrida, Jacques. 'To Do Justice to Freud.' *Resistances of Psychoanalysis*. Transl. Peggy Kamuf. Stanford: CA: Stanford University Press, 1998: 70–118.

Desert Storm Indymedia. 2002. Web. December 2004. <http://antimedia.net/desertstorm/>.

Dominijanni, Ida. 'From the Italian Laboratory of the 1970s to the Global Laboratory of a Politics Opposed to Forms of War.' *Aut-op-sy mailing list archive,* 4 October 2004. Web. October 2005. <http://archives.econ.utah.edu/archives/aut-op-sy/2004m10/msg00019.htm>.

Duden Deutsches Universalworterbuch. Second edition. Mannheim: Duden Verlag, 1989.

Eagleton, Terry. 'The Enlightenment Is Dead! Long Live the Enlightenment!' *Harper's Magazine,* March 2005. New York: Harper's Magazine, 2005: 91–95.

Edgar, Andrew, and Peter Sedgwick. *Cultural Theory: The Key Concepts.* London and New York: Routledge, 2002.

Electronic Frontier Foundation. Defending Freedom in the Digital World, n.d. Web. March 2004. <http://www.eff.org/>.

Eisenstein, Zillah. *Global Obscenities: Patriarchy, Capitalism, and the Lure of Cyberfantasy.* New York: New York University Press, 1998.

European Research Centre on Migration and Ethnic Relations, n.d. Web. November 2005. <http://www.uu.nl/uupublish/onderzoek/onderzoekcentra/ercomer/24638main.html>.

'Expressionismus.' *Literaturepochen,* n.d. Web. June 2006. <http://members.aon.at/livingbox/expressionismus.html>.

Facoltà di Fuga. 'EU Free and Self-Governing European University.' *rekombinant* mail-archive. 3 February 2003. Web. July 2005. <http://www.mail-archive.com/rekombinant@autistici.org/msg00355.html>.

Fadil, Nadia. 'De hersenschim van de onderdrukte moslimvrouw.' *Indymedia Belgium,* 3 May 2003. Web. March 2004. <http://belgium.indymedia.org/news/2003/05/60732_comment.php#60770>.

Foster, Wayne. 'Border Camps: The New "Sexy" Thing?' *Greenpepper Magazine.* December 2002. Web. June 2005. <http://squat.net/cia/gp/hom3c.php?artid=141&back=/cia/gp/hom.php>.

Garcia, Neil. 'Performativity, the *Bakla*, and the Orientalising Gaze.' *Inter-Asia Cultural Studies* 1.2, August (2000): 265–281.

Gills, Barry K. *Globalization and the Politics of Resistance.* London: Macmillan Press, 2000.

'Give Up Activism.' *Do or Die,* issue 9, 2001. Web. June 2005. <http://www.eco-action.org/dod/no9/activism.htm>.

Glocal Research Space. 'Activist Research.' *Greenpepper.* Winter 2003. Web. July 2005. http://www.mucolin.de/gp-03–04/PDF/gp_03–04_empire-articles.pdf.

Goddard, Anne. 'Woomera 2002.' 2003. Web. October 2004. <http://library.sievxmemorial.org/agoddard001.htm>.

Gore, Al. *An Inconvenient Truth.* Dir. Davis Guggenheim. 2006. Film.

Grosz, Elizabeth. 'Ontology and Equivocation. Derrida's Politics of Sexual Difference.' *Feminist Interpretations of Jacques Derrida.* Ed. Nancy Holland. University Park: Pennsylvania State University Press, 1997: 73–102.

Halleck, DeeDee. 'Gathering Storm: The Open Cyber Forum of Indymedia.' Paper presented at *Our Media Not Theirs* conference. Barcelona, Spain, July 2002. Web. January 2005. <http://www.ourmedianet.org/om2002/papers2002/Halleck.IAMCR2002.pdf>.

Haraway, Donna. 'A Cyborg Manifesto: Science, Technology and Socialist-Feminism in the Late Twentieth Century.' *Simians, Cyborgs and Women: The Reinvention of Nature.* New York: Routledge, 1991: 149–182.

Haraway, Donna. 'Situated Knowledges: The Science Question in Feminism and the Privilege of Partial Perspective.' *Feminism and Science.* Ed. Evelyn Fox-Keller and Helen Longino. Oxford: Oxford University Press, 1996: 249–263.

Hardt, Michael, and Antonio Negri. *Empire.* Cambridge, MA: Harvard University Press, 2000.

Hardt, Michael, and Antonio Negri. *Multitude: War and Democracy in the Age of Empire.* New York: Penguin Press, 2004.

Harris, Paul G. *World Ethics and Climate Change: From International to Global Justice.* Edinburgh: Edinburgh University Press, 2010.

Heidegger, Martin. 'Letter on Humanism.' *From Modernism to Postmodernism: An Anthology.* Ed. L. Cahoone. Cambridge, MA: Blackwell Publishers, 1996: 274–308.

Heidegger, Martin. 'The Question Concerning Technology.' *Basic Writings from Being and Time to the Task of Thinking.* Ed. David Farrell Krell. New York: HarperCollins Publishers, 1977: 307–342.

Heimbuch, Jaymi. 'Arguing with a Climate Change Skeptic? There's an App for That.' 11 February 2011. Web. <http://www.treehugger.com/clean-technology/arguing-with-a-climate-change-skeptic-theres-an-app-for-that.html>.

HelpB92, n.d. Web. November 2005. <http://helpb92.xs4all.nl/>.

Henshaw-Plath, Evan. 'Email Interview about Indymedia Tech Vision.' *Mediapolitics Archives,* 1 November 2001. Web. June 2007. <http://archives.lists.indymedia.org/mediapolitics/2001-November/000041.html>.

Hoofd, Ingrid. 'Indymedia Debate @ N5M4.' *The IMC-Europe Archives,* 19 September 2003. Web. March 2010. <http://lists.indymedia.org/pipermail/imc-europe/2003-September/001511.html>.

Hudson, David. 'Re: Gandhis running amok.' *OpenMute,* 2002. Web. June 2005. <http://docs.metamute.com/view/Open/OrganisationalStructures>.

Ignatow, Gabriel. *Transnational Identity Politics and the Environment.* New York: Rowman & Littlefield Publishers, 2007.

Illich, Fran: 'Ready to Delete the Border.' *MakeWorlds,* 4 July 2004. Web. May 2008. <http://www.makeworlds.org/node/134>.

'IMC UK Mission Statement.' *Indymedia UK,* n.d. Web. March 2004. <http://www.indymedia.org.uk/en/static/mission.html>.

'Indymedia Debate @ n5m.' *Indymedia Documentation Project.* September 2003. Web. December 2003. <http://docs.indymedia.org/view/Global/NextFiveMinutes>.

'Indymedia: Don't Hate the Media, Be the Media,' 'Indymedia: Precursors and Birth,' and 'Indymedia: Who Are We?' *We Are Everywhere: The Irresistible Rise of Global Anticapitalism.* Ed. Notes from Nowhere. London: Verso, 2003: 228–243.

'Indymedia's Frequently Asked Questions.' *Indymedia Documentation Project,* n.d. Web. January 2004. <http://docs.indymedia.org/view/Global/FrequentlyAskedQuestionEn>.

International Office of Migration, n.d. Web. November 2009. <http://www.iom.int/>.

Investigació. '1st International Conference on Social Movements and Activist Research.' December 2004. Web. May 2005. <http://www.investigaccio.org/>.

Jordan, Tim. 'Ethics, Activisms, Futures.' *Activism! Direct Action, Hacktivism and the Future of Society.* London: Reaktion Books, 2002: 137–156.

Juris, Jeffrey. 'Indymedia: From Counter-Information to Informational Utopics.' *Investigació: Jornades Recerca Activista.* 2004. Web. June 2009. <http://www.investigaccio.org/ponencies/juris3.pdf>.

Juris, Jeffrey. 'The New Digital Media and Activist Networking within Anti-Corporate Globalization Movements.' *The Anthropology of Globalization: A Reader.* Ed. Jonathan Xavier Inda and Renato Rosaldo. Malden, MA: Blackwell Publishers, 2008: 352–372.

Juris, Jeffrey. *Networking Futures: The Movements against Corporate Globalization.* Durham, NC: Duke University Press, 2008.

Kamuf, Peggy. 'Deconstruction and Feminism: A Repetition.' *Feminist Interpretations of Jacques Derrida.* Ed. Nancy Holland. University Park: Pennsylvania State University Press, 1997: 103–126.

Kamuf, Peggy. 'Violence, Identity, Self-Determination, and the Question of Justice: On *Specters of Marx.*' *Violence, Identity and Self-Determination.* Ed. Hent De Vries, H. and Samuel Weber. Stanford, CA: Stanford University Press, 1997: 271–283.

Kamuf, Peggy. 'Deconstruction and Love.' *Deconstructions: A User's Guide.* Ed. Nicholas Royle. Hampshire, UK: Palgrave, 2000: 151–170.

Katsiaficas, George. 'Italian Autonomia.' *The Subversion of Politics: European Autonomous Movements and the Decolonization of Everyday Life.* Atlantic Highlands, NJ: Humanities Press International, 1997: 18–58.

Kein Mench Ist Illegal. 2005. Web. March 2007. < http://www.kmii-koeln.de>.

Kellner, Douglas. *Jean Baudrillard: From Marxism to Postmodernism and Beyond.* Stanford, CA: Stanford University Press, 1989.

Kidd, Dorothy. 'Indymedia.org. A New Communication Commons.' *Cyberactivisms. Online Activism in Theory and Practice.* Ed. Martha McCaughey and Michael D. Ayers. New York: Routledge, 2003: 47–70.

Klein, Naomi. 'A New Climate Movement in Bolivia.' *The Nation,* 22 April 2010. Web. June 2010. http://www.thenation.com/print/article/new-climate-movement-bolivia.

Koomey, Jonathan. 'Estimating Total Power Consumption by Servers in the U.S. and the World.' 15 February 2007. Web. October 2010. <http://sites.amd.com/us/Documents/svrpwrusecompletefinal.pdf>.

Laclau, Ernesto, and Chantal Mouffe. *Hegemony and Socialist Strategy: Towards a Radical Democratic Politics.* Transl. Winston Moore and Paul Cammack. London: Verso, 1985.

Lewis, Kanthi. 'Civil Disobedience and Woomera.' *The UTS website,* n.d. Web. February 2006. <http://www.international.activism.uts.edu.au/conferences/civildis/lewis.html>.

Lovink, Geert. 'Network Fears and Desires.' *Dark Fiber. Tracking Critical Internet Culture.* Cambridge, MA: MIT Press, 2002: 226–233.

Lovink, Geert. 'The Technology of News.' *Subsol,* December 2002. Web. June 2008. <http://subsol.c3.hu/subsol_2/contributors3/lovinktext2.html>.

Lovink, Geert, and Florian Schneider. 'A Virtual World Is Possible: From Tactical Media to Digital Multitudes.' *Artnodes. Intersections between Arts, Sciences and Technologies,* 2003. Web. February 2009. <http://www.uoc.edu/artnodes/espai/eng/art/lovink_schneider0603/lovink_schneider0603.pdf>.

Lovink, Geert, and Florian Schneider. 'Reverse Engineering Freedom.' *MakeWorlds,* 21 September 2003. Web. May 2009. <http://makeworlds.net/node/20>.

Lovink, Geert, and Gayatri Spivak. 'Pax Electronica: Against Crisis-Driven Global Telecommunication.' *Uncanny Networks. Dialogues with the Virtual Intelligentsia.* Ed. Geert Lovink. Cambridge, MA: MIT Press, 2002: 74–81.

Lovink, Geert, and Soenke Zehle. 'Incommunicado: Information Technology for Everybody Else.' 2005. Web. October 2005. <http://www.incommunicado.info/>.

Maguire, John. 'The Tears inside the Stone.' *Risk, Environment and Modernity: Towards a New Ecology.* Ed. Scott Lash, Bronislaw Szerszynski, and Brian Wynne. London: Sage, 1996: 169–188.

Martin, Fran. 'Dismembering Theory: Working Notes.' *The Department of English at NCU Taiwan,* 2004. Web. March 2005. <http://www.ncu.edu.tw/~eng/journal/journal_park12.htm>.

Mauzz. 'Re: wijlen het globale Indymedianetwerk?' *IMC-Netherlands Editorial Archive.* imc-nl-editorial@indymedia.nl (18 May 2005).

'MDI doet aangifte tegen Indymedia NL.' *Indymedia.NL (Nederland),* 2 October 2002. Web. February 2004. <http://indymedia.nl/nl/2002/10/6738.shtml>.

Mezzadra, Sandro, and Fabio Raimondi. 'Van mondiale beweging naar multitude.' *Globalinfo*, 29 April 2002. Web. July 2010. <http://www.globalinfo.nl/Achter-grond/van-mondiale-beweging-naar-multitude.html>.

Mezzadra, Sandro. 'Citizenship in Motion.' *MakeWorlds*, 22 February 2004. Web. August 2009. <http://makeworlds.net/node/83>.

Mezzadra, Sandro. 'The Right to Escape.' *Ephemera—Theory of the Multitude*, 4.3, 2004: 267–275. Web. July 2004. <http://www.ephemeraweb.org/journal/4–3/4–3mezzadra.pdf>.

Mitropoulos, Angela. 'Flotilla of Hope Update.' *Indymedia Sydney*, 2004. Web. August 2004. <http://sydney.indymedia.org/front.php3?article_id=41985>.

Mitropoulos, Angela. 'Movements against the Enclosures: Virtual Is Preamble.' *MakeWorlds*, 7 April 2004. Web. July 2004. <http://www.makeworlds.org/node/133>.

Mitropoulos, Angela. 'The Micro-Physics of Theoretical Production and Border Crossings.' *Borderlands*, vol. 3, No. 2, 2004. Web. August 2008. <http://www.borderlandsejournal.adelaide.edu.au/vol3no2_2004/mitropoulos_microphysics.htm>.

Mobilized Investigation. 'Mission Statement,' 2003. Web. April 2005. <http://manifestor.org/mi/en/2003/01/13.shtml>.

Morozov, Evgeny. *The Net Delusion: The Dark Side of Internet Freedom*. New York: Public Affairs, 2011.

Mouffe, Chantal. 'Radical Democracy or Liberal Democracy?' *Radical Democracy: Identity, Citizenship, and the State*. Ed. David Trend. New York: Routledge, 1996: 19–26.

Nakamura, Lisa. 'Interrogating the Digital Divide: The Political Economy of Race and Commerce in New Media.' *Society Online: The Internet in Context*. Ed. Philip N. Howard and Steve Jones. Thousand Oaks, CA: Sage, 2004: 71–86.

Negri, Antonio, and Danilo Zolo. 'Empire and the Multitude. A Dialogue on the New Order of Globalisation.' *Generation-online*, 2002. Web. July 2009. <http://www.generation-online.org/t/empiremultitude.htm>.

Negri, Antonio. 'M as in Multitude.' *Negri on Negri: Antonio Negri in Conversation with Anne Dufourmantelle*. London: Routledge, 2004: 111–118.

Neilson, Brett. 'Italy in Translation: Radical Thought Dislocated to the Antipodes.' *Aut-op-sy mailing list archive*. 4 October 2004. Web. October 2005. <http://archives.econ.utah.edu/archives/aut-op-sy/2004m10/msg00019.htm>.

Neilson, Brett. 'Neither Here or Elsewhere. Interview with Sandro Mezzadra.' *MakeWorlds–Neuro—Networking Europe*, 21 September 2003. Web. November 2010. <http://makeworlds.net/node/17>.

Next Five Minutes International Festival of Tactical Media, n.d. Web. March 2005. <http://www.next5minutes.org/index.jsp>.

Nigam, Aditya. 'The Old Left in a New World: The Mumbai Resistance?' E-mail on undercurrents@bbs.thing.net (24 December 2003).

Nik. 'Personal Account from the Woomera 2002 Protests in Australia.' *Nettime*. 4 April 2002. Web. October 2007. <http://amsterdam.nettime.org/Lists-Archives/nettime-bold-0204/msg00106.html>.

No-Border Network, n.d. Web. September 2004. <http://www.no-border.org/news_index.php>.

'No Borders, No Nations.' *We Are Everywhere: The Irresistible Rise of Global Anticapitalism*. Ed. Notes from Nowhere. London: Verso, 2003: 428–429.

Noonan, Jeff. *Critical Humanism and the Politics of Difference*. Montreal: McGill-Queens University Press, 2003.

Norris, Christopher. *Uncritical Theory: Postmodernism, Intellectuals, and the Gulf War*. London: Lawrence and Wishart, 1992.

Nussbaum, Martha. 'The Professor of Parody.' *The New Republic Online*, 22 February 1999: 37–45. Web. August 2010. <http://www.akad.se/Nussbaum.pdf>.

'NYC IMC Adopts Moderation For Their Newswire.' *Indymedia.NYC (New York City)*. 3 July 2003. Web. September 2010. <http://lists.indymedia.org/pipermail/imc-sc/2003-July/001662.html>.

Obadiah. 'Woomera Tales.' *Aut-op-sy mailing list archive*. April 2004. Web. August 2004. <http://archives.econ.utah.edu/archives/aut-op-sy/2002m04/msg00016.htm>.

'Open Publishing, Editorial Policy, Decision Making.' *Pittsburgh Independent Media Centre*, n.d. Web. March 2004. <http://pittsburgh.indymedia.org/process/openpub.php>.

Pasquinelli, Matteo. 'Radical Machines against the Techno-Empire.' *Rekombinant.org*, 2004. Web. August 2004. <http://www.rekombinant.org/article.php?sid=2264>.

Partridge, Eric. *Origins: An Etymological Dictionary of Modern English*. London: Routledge, 1990.

Pavis, Theta. 'The Rise of the Indymedia Movement.' *Online Journalism Review*. January 2002. Web. April 2005. <http://www.cb3rob.net/~merijn89/ARCH2/msg00013.html>.

Perlstein, Jeff. 'The Independent Media Center Movement.' *MediaAlliance*, 2003. Web. April 2005. <http://www.media-alliance.org/article.php?story=20031109003144928&query=perlstein>.

Platon, Sara, and Mark Deuze. 'Indymedia Journalism: A Radical Way of Making, Selecting and Sharing News?' *Journalism* 4.3, Sage (2003): 336–355.

Ponzanesi, Sandra. 'Diasporic Subjects and Migration.' *Thinking Differently: A Reader in European Women's Studies*. Ed. Gabrielle Griffin and Rosi Braidotti. London: Zed Books, 2002: 205–220.

'Principles of Unity.' *Indymedia Documentation Project*, n.d. Web. November 2003. <http://docs.indymedia.org/view/Global/PrinciplesOfUnity>.

Rambatan, Bonnie. 'Are Trees the New Proletariat?' *Cyborg Subjects Online Journal*. September 2010. Web. October 2010. <http://journal.cyborgsubjects.org/2010/09/trees-proletariat/>.

Readings, Bill. 'Theory after Theory. Institutional Questions.' *The Politics of Research*. Ed. E. Ann Kaplan and George Levine. New Brunswick, NJ: Rutgers University Press, 1997: 21–33.

Rete Nationale Ricercatori Precari. 'Globalisation, Academic Flexibility and the Right to Research: A Call for a European Network of Precarious/Temporary Researchers and for the Free Circulation of Knowledge,' 2005. Web. August 2005. http://www.euromovements.info/html/xarca-precaris-it.htm.

Richardson, Joanne. 'The Language of Tactical Media.' *Sarai Reader 2003: Shaping Technologies*, 2003. Web. March 2010. <http://www.sarai.net/publications/readers/03-shaping-technologies/346_351_jrichardson.pdf>.

Robbins, Bruce. 'Oppositional Professionals: Theory and the Narratives of Professionalisation.' *Consequences of Theory*. Ed. Jonathan Arac and Barbara Johnson. Baltimore: Johns Hopkins University Press, 1991.

Rustin, Michael. 'Empire: A Postmodern Theory of Revolution.' *Debating Empire*. Ed. Gopal Balakrishnan. London: Verso, 2003: 1–25.

Ryan, Michael. 'The Theory of Autonomy.' *Politics and Culture: Working Hypotheses for a Post-Revolutionary Society*. London: Macmillan Press, 1989.

Schultz, Pit: 'Pit Schultz Interview with Paul Garrin.' *Nettime* 13. June 1997. Web. November 2005. <http://www.nettime.org/Lists-Archives/nettime-l-9706/msg00094.html>.

Shaw, Martin. 'A Question to Jacques Derrida,' 1997. Web. July 2005. <http://www.sussex.ac.uk/Users/hafa3/derrida.htm>.

Shukman, David. 'Glacier Threat to Bolivia Capital.' *BBC Science and Environment*, 4 December 2009. Web. January 2010. <http://news.bbc.co.uk/2/hi/8394324.stm>.

Soper, Kate. 'Nature/"Nature".' Ed. George Robertson et. al. *FutureNatural: Nature, Science, Culture*. London: Routledge, 1996: 22–34.

Spivak, Gayatri Chakravorty. 'Marginality in the Teaching Machine.' *Outside in the Teaching Machine*. London/New York: Routledge, 1993: 53–76.

Spivak, Gayatri Chakravorty. 'Practical Politics of the Open End.' *The Post-Colonial Critic: Interviews, Strategies, Dialogues*. Ed. Sarah Harasym. New York: Routledge, 1990: 95–112.

Spivak, Gayatri Chakravorty. *A Critique of Postcolonial Reason: Toward a History of the Vanishing Present*. Cambridge, MA: Harvard University Press, 1999.

Spivak, Gayatri Chakravorty. 'In the New World Order: A Speech.' *Marxism in the Postmodern Age*. Ed. Antonio Callari, Stephen Cullenberg, and Carole Biewener. New York: The Guilford Press, 1995: 89–99.

Spivak, Gayatri Chakravorty. 'Revolutions That as Yet Have No Model: Derrida's "Limited Inc." ' *The Spivak Reader*. Ed. Donna Landry and Gerald MacLean. New York: Routledge, 1991: 75–106.

Spivak, Gayatri Chakravorti, and Mary Zournazi. 'The Rest of the World.' *Hope: New Philosophies for Change*. Ed. Mary Zournazi. New York: Routledge, 2002: 172–190.

Spivak, Gayatri Chakravorty, and David Plotke. 'A Dialogue on Democracy.' *Radical Democracy: Identity, Citizenship, and the State*. Ed. David Trend. New York: Routledge, 1996: 209–222.

Spivak, Gayatri Chakravorty, and Elizabeth Grosz. 'Criticism, Feminism and the Institution.' *The Post-Colonial Critic: Interviews, Strategies, Dialogues*. Ed. Sarah Harasym. New York: Routledge, 1990: 1–16.

Sullivan, Sian. 'Barcelona 22–25 January 2004: First International Conference on Social Movements and Activism,' 2004. Web. July 2005. <http://www.euromovements.info/html/sian-investigaccio.htm>.

Swyngedouw, Erik. 'Apocalypse Forever? Post-Political Populism and the Spectre of Climate Change.' *Theory, Culture and Society* 27.2–3, 2010: 213–232.

Szerszynski, Bronislaw. 'On Knowing What to Do: Environmentalism and the Modern Problematic.' *Risk, Environment and Modernity: Towards a New Ecology*. Ed. Scott Lash, Bronislaw Szerszynski, and Brain Wynne. London: Sage, 1996: 104–138.

The IMC—A New Model: The Indymedia Documentation Project, 2004. Web. April 2004. <http://docs.indymedia.org/view/Global/FirstEditionOfINDYMEDIAHANDBOOK>.

'The Indymedia Debate.' *Next Five Minutes 4 Festival of Tactical Media*. Amsterdam, 11–14 September 2003. Web. February 2004. <http://www.next5minutes.org/n5m/article.jsp?articleid=1712>.

Treanor, Paul. 'Neoliberalism: Origins, Theory, Definition.' 2 December 2005. Web. October 2009. <http://web.inter.nl.net/users/Paul.Treanor/neoliberalism.html>.

Van Aalst, Peter, and Stefaan Walgrave. 'New Media, New Movements? The Role of the Internet in Shaping the "Anti-Globalization" Movement.' *Cyberprotest: New Media, Citizens, and Social Movements*. Ed. Wim van de Donk et. al. New York: Routledge, 2004: 87–108.

Van de Donk, Wim, Brian Loader, Paul Nixon, and Dieter Rucht. *Cyberprotest: New Media, Citizens, and Social Movements*. New York: Routledge, 2004.

Van Loon, Joost. 'Mediating the Risks of Virtual Environments.' *Environmental Risk and the Media*. Ed. Stuart Allan, Barbara Adam, and Cynthia Carter. London: Routledge, 2000: 129–140.

Vidal, John, Allegra Stratton, and Suzanne Goldenberg. 'Low Targets, Goals Dropped: Copenhagen Ends in Failure.' *The Guardian*, 19 December 2009. Web. March 2010. <http://www.guardian.co.uk/environment/2009/dec/18/copenhagen-deal>.

Virno, Paolo. 'Virtuosity and Revolution: The Political Theory of Exodus.' *Radical Thought in Italy: A Potential Politics*. Ed. Paolo Virno and Michael Hardt. Minneapolis: University of Minnesota Press, 1996: 189–212.

Virilio, Paul. *The Original Accident*. Cambridge: Polity Press, 2007.

Virilio, Paul. *War and Cinema: The Logistics of Perception*. Transl. Patrick Camiller. London: Verso, 1989.

Virilio, Paul, and Louise Wilson. 'Cyberwar, God and Television: Interview with Paul Virilio.' *Electronic Culture*. Ed. Timothy Druckrey. New York: Aperture, 1996: 121–130.

Virilio, Paul. 'The Museum of Accidents.' Transl. Chris Turner. *International Journal of Baudrillard Studies* 3.2, July 2006. Web. October 2009. <http://www.ubishops.ca/baudrillardstudies/vol3_2/virilio.htm>.

Virilio, Paul, and Sylvère Lotringer. *Pure War*. New York: Semiotext(e), 2008.

Virno, Paolo, and Michael Hardt. *Radical Thought in Italy: A Potential Politics*. Minneapolis: University of Minnesota Press, 1996.

Waltz, Mitzi. *Alternative and Activist Media*. Edinburgh: Edinburgh University Press, 2005.

'Was ist Indymedia?' *Indymedia Germany,* n.d. Web. March 2008. <http://germany.indymedia.org/static/ms.shtml>.

West, Cornel. 'Theory, Pragmatism, and Politics.' *Consequences of Theory*. Ed. Jonathan Arac and Barbara Johnson. Baltimore: Johns Hopkins University Press, 1991: 22–38.

White, Jess. 'Restore the Commons! Break the Borders!' *Greenpepper Magazine*. December 2002. Web. July 2005. <http://squat.net/cia/gp/hom3c.php?artid=157&back=/cia/gp/hom.php>.

White, Jess. 'We Are Human Beings: The Woomera Breakout.' *We Are Everywhere: The Irresistible Rise of Global Anticapitalism*. Ed. Notes from Nowhere. London: Verso, 2003: 430–436.

Wilkie, Rob. 'The Daydreams of iPod Capitalism.' *The Red Critique* No.10, Spring 2005. Web. March 2009. <http://www.redcritique.org/WinterSpring2005/thedaydreamsofipodcapitalism.htm>.

Wills, David. 'Techneology or the Discourse of Speed.' *The Prosthetic Impulse: From a Posthuman Present to a Biocultural Future*. Ed. Marquard Smith and Joanne Morra. Cambridge, MA: MIT Press, 2006: 237–263.

Wilson, Kris M. 'Communicating Climate Change through the Media: Predictions, Politics and Perceptions of Risk.' *Environmental Risks and the Media*. Ed. Stuart Allan, Barbara Adam, and Cynthia Carter. London: Routledge, 2000: 201–217.

Woomera2002. 2002. Web. September 2004. <http://woomera2002.antimedia.net/>.

World Bank Institute. 'Apps for Climate.' Web. November 2011. <https://wbchallenge.imaginatik.com/wbchallengecomp.nsf/x/competition?open&eid=201111 1685257879005955D51068264>.

World People's Conference on Climate Change and the Rights of Mother Earth. 'Rights of Mother Earth,' n.d. Web. September 2010. <http://pwccc.wordpress.com/programa/>.

x-border. 2004. Web. August 2009. <http://www.antimedia.net/xborder/>.

Žižek, Slavoj. 'A Symptom—of What?' *Critical Inquiry* 29.3, Spring, 2003: 486–503.

Index

For Product Safety Concerns and Information please contact our EU
representative GPSR@taylorandfrancis.com
Taylor & Francis Verlag GmbH, Kaufingerstraße 24, 80331 München, Germany

www.ingramcontent.com/pod-product-compliance
Ingram Content Group UK Ltd.
Pitfield, Milton Keynes, MK11 3LW, UK
UKHW020945180425
457613UK00019B/524